# THE STUDY OF LANGUAGES

BROUGHT BACK TO ITS TRUE PRINCIPLES,

OR THE

## ART OF THINKING IN A FOREIGN LANGUAGE.

BY

MARCEL, Knt. Leg. Hon.,

AUTHOR OF "LANGUAGE AS A MEANS OF MENTAL CULTURE," ETC.; "PREMIERS PRINCIPES D'EDUCATION," ETC., ETC.

> "La nature a fait ce système elle-même; elle pouvait seule le faire."
>
> CONDILLAC.
>
> "Les méthodes sont les maîtres des maîtres."
>
> TALLEYRAND.

NEW YORK:
D. APPLETON AND COMPANY,
90, 92 & 94 GRAND STREET.
1869.

## NOTE TO THE AMERICAN EDITION.

The great want of an American in travelling abroad is not so much the ability to speak the language of the country which he may visit, as to understand it when spoken by the natives. He may fancy that his knowledge of the written language will stand him in good stead for purposes of business or social intercourse, but his first attempt at practical conversation will undeceive him. He may manage to express himself in decent French or German, but the responses of his interlocutor will be as unintelligible as Sanscrit or Choctaw. He has learned the language by the eye, but not by the ear. The same words which he reads and translates at sight fail to be recognized when they fall from the lips. He finds that his habit of reading gives him no power to understand talking. Even the most familiar phrases address his eye and ear so differently, that they have a strange and unmeaning sound when spoken. Of the American travellers who crowd the foreign capitals at all seasons, few have sufficient mastery of the European languages to be able to carry on a connected conversation, though they have no trouble in understanding the language of books. One may be well grounded in the literature of a language, reading the works of its authors with as great ease as he does his own vernacular, and still, on attempting to converse with a native, will find himself as helpless as a child. The fault is not in his knowledge, but in his ear. He may even be able to speak with a certain rash fluency, but he breaks down in trying to understand what is said to him. The sound of the words with which his eye is familiar conveys no sense to his ear. In a great majority of cases this is the cause of the inability of a stranger, who has studied a foreign language in books, to apply it to practical use. The perusal of a thousand volumes would not enable the student to understand a single word of the spoken language. In the brief essay now offered to the public, of which a French edition was published in 1867, a method of learning foreign languages is proposed, which affords an effectual remedy for the evil referred to. The author is a French scholar of rare philosophical culture and linguistic accomplishments, who for many years has pursued the method in his own studies which he recommends to his readers. His success is brilliantly illustrated by the vigor and idiomatic purity which mark the composition of this volume. He handles the English language with the force and precision of a native writer, and often awakens an interest in his ideas by the simple beauty of his style. His little work is not a manual, but a method. Though devoted to the study of language as a subject of philosophical investigation, he has never been a teacher.] His method is equally applicable to the different systems on which text-books have been written. Its principal features may be described in a concise summary as follows: 1. Every exercise leads to the power of thinking in the language. 2. Nature is followed, step by step, through the study. 3. Curiosity and imitation are the sources of progress. 4. Grammar is learned through the language. 5. Every exercise is in itself a lesson in the practice of the language. 6. Exercises in translating into the foreign language are not demanded of the beginner. 7. The phraseology is known before the words. 8. No lesson is learned by rote. 9. Pronunciation is learned through the ear alone. 10. The language, when spoken however fast, is perfectly understood. 11. All the exercises provide against the commission of errors. 12. An instructor is required only for the pronunciation.

In the application of this method the ear is trained before the pupil attempts to speak, following the wonderful process of nature, by which the infant goes through a varied course of auricular exercises, before the tongue is called into action. The ultimate aim is to give a complete command of the language, whether spoken or written, without the medium of a translation.

Every one who learns a foreign language, according to this method, will be able to apply its resources, both for thought and speech, with the certainty, if not the facility, of his native tongue. In his travels abroad, he can join in social intercourse with ease and pleasure, instead of being tied down to the lifeless routine of the written language. Without this faculty, though he may have turned night into day in the study of the national literature, it will still be true of him, that "he who travelleth into a country before he hath some entrance into the language, goeth to school, and not to travel."

# PREFACE.

Civilization is the offspring of the social sentiment: men of all countries, impelled by an instinct of perfectibility, come daily into closer contact, desirous of communicating, of assimilating with each other in social intercourse. The old barriers which ignorance and national prejudice had raised between them are now crumbling in every direction before the irresistible power of that instinct.

International exchange of ideas is the great want of the age. With a view to supplying this want, we have endeavored to render the knowledge of foreign living languages accessible to every one by taking for our guide the natural method by which all so infalliby acquire their native tongue. Our system is formed of what is conformable to reason and sanctioned by experience in the labors of our predecessors. It will be found consistent with the working of the mind, the nature of language, and the requirements of modern society.

The present diversity of methods in this branch of instruction sufficiently proves that they are not founded on sound, universal principles: they are partial and exclusive. There is something true in each, but none contain the whole truth: this remains to be discovered. For our own part, we shall rest satisfied if we throw some light on the subject, and if, by taking a few steps toward its amelioration, we prepare the way for its future perfection.

This attempt of one not a teacher may be deemed presumptuous: the only excuse we can offer is our wish to be useful; and we doubt not we shall be so, especially to those of our readers who are ambitious to know a foreign language practically, and to those who, unbiassed by any previous routine, are entering upon the career of instruction.

Special directions are given for the acquisition of ancient and modern languages, whether the learner be a child or an adult, a beginner or a proficient, whether he learns with or without a teacher, in private or in a class; while the classification of the subject will permit every person to direct his attention to the object best suited to his wants.

The highest ability in the various departments of the language is insisted upon. Perfection, it is true, is unattainable; but the purport of a method, as the duty of an instructor, is to keep it always in perspective before young people, and to lead them toward it, as far as circumstances permit.

The present volume is a brief summary of a larger work, in which all our views on linguistic studies are unfolded at full length.*

C. M.

Paris, *December*, 1868.

* "Language as a Means of Mental Culture and International Communication." 2 vols., 8vo. London: Chapman & Hall. 1853.

# CONTENTS.

# THE STUDY OF LANGUAGES,

*BROUGHT BACK TO ITS TRUE PRINCIPLES.*

---

## CHAPTER I.

### SUBDIVISION AND ORDER OF STUDY.

"The order which a good classification introduces into our studies, throws light on them, and insures their rapid progress."

Before unfolding the method which is the subject of this essay, we will briefly indicate the objects which it embraces, and the principles on which it rests. Classification is the basis of a rational method.

Man, born with a social nature, is endowed with the means of entering into communion with his fellow-creatures. His looks, smiles, laughter, tears, cries, sighs, gestures, all the changes of his countenance, all the intonations of his voice, all muscular actions, the immediate consequence of impressions received, are the natural signs which manifest externally his emotions, his sentiments.

They constitute *the language of action.* Through these signs, men of all countries can communicate with each other, and the young child is able to understand those who address him.

Expressive, however, as this language of nature is, it was found inadequate for all the wants of active and social life in an advanced state of civilization. Its deficiencies and the increasing demand for intellectual communication soon led to *articulate language*, which, although arising from the spontaneous action of our faculties, is of human institution and composed of conventional signs.

In process of time and with the further progress of civilization, articulate language became insufficient, as it exercised its power in narrow limits of time and place, and *written language* was invented. With speech alone, nations, provinces, towns would have remained isolated; generations would have succeeded generations without deriving benefit from their experience; in a word, mankind would have remained in a comparative state of ignorance.

The conventional signs of our ideas are then of two sorts—*spoken* and *written words.*

Spoken words are composed of two elements

—*vocal sounds* and *vocal articulations.* The combination of the two forms the *articulate sound.*

Written words are likewise composed of two elements corresponding to those of the spoken words; they are the *vowels* and *consonants,* which represent respectively the sounds and articulations.

Such is the double system of signs, the knowledge of which is required for the exchange of ideas.

In the study of a living language, four ends are to be attained, that is, four different arts, which we give here in the order of their acquisition in the mother tongue:

1. To understand the spoken language.
2. To speak.
3. To understand the written language.
4. To write.

The first two arts, constitute the *spoken language;* the other two, the *written language.* The former is acquired naturally, the latter must be taught.

The language of action which accompanies the first words addressed to a child, interprets their meaning, and intuitively fixes the idea in his mind; thus, under the impulse of nature alone he directly associates ideas with the phraseology which strikes his ear, without even suspecting that it is composed of words. By a wise provision of the Creator, which compels him to be mute at his entrance into life, the child, prompted by curiosity, silently exercises his perceptive powers and listens to all around him. When his organ of hearing is completely familiarized with the articulate sounds to which he attaches ideas, he instinctively reproduces these sounds, in order to express his desires, his wants, his thoughts. Here spontaneity ceases. If we wish him to know how to read and write, he must be taught.

To possess these four objects, is to be able to use the *spoken* and the *written* words, for either receiving or communicating ideas. This exchange of thought is efficient only when words exist in the mind as direct representatives of ideas, when, alternately cause and effect, they spontaneously suggest each other: in other words, when we think in the language. The child thinks with the very first words which he stammers.

There are four ways of thinking in a language, corresponding to the four ways of practising it. They are the four objects to be attained in succession, and so far distinct, that the possession of one does not necessarily imply the possession of the others. They are manifested by the action of different organs, and supply different social wants. Completely dissimilar in the end proposed and in actual practice, although connected by close affinities, these objects require for their attainment special exercises, in conformity with the process of nature, and in such an order that each may be a preparation for that which is to follow. As they are successively rendered habitual by practice, the spontaneity with which every one of them is exercised, leaves all the powers of the mind free to make the other acquisitions, without neglecting those which precede. Thus, by dividing the difficulties, we are enabled to surmount them. One thing at a time, and every thing in its time: these are the prescriptions of nature and reason.

The order to be followed in the pursuit of these acquisitions is indicated by the degree of importance belonging to each, and the subserviency of some to the others. Ideas are not innate; they must be received before they can be communicated; this is so true, that native curiosity impels us to listen long before we can speak.

A child instinctively follows this order; he does not waste his mental activity on vain theories; he goes straight to the phraseology; he listens and understands; he imitates and speaks.

It is only when the articulate sounds spontaneously awaken in his young intelligence the ideas of which they are the signs, that he tries to reproduce them as he has heard them. He owes his progress to *example*, not to precepts; to *practice*, not to theory.

This is analysis, the method of nature: based on example and practice, it proceeds, by induction, from the perceptions to their signs, from the whole to its parts, from the phraseology to the words, from the forms of language to the laws that govern them.

It is under the impulse of these instincts of nature that we infallibly acquire the language of our parents. The same process, applied to any other language, must produce the same result; and success will be the more certain, as we follow more closely in the steps of nature.

The articulate and the written signs being conventional, a familiarity with the import attached to them must be gained before they can be properly applied to the expression of thought. It is only after ideas have been conveyed to our minds by means of their signs, that we can, by imitation, use these very signs to express the same or similar ideas. IMPRESSION of language, which is effected through *hearing* and *reading*, must therefore precede EXPRESSION, which is effected by *speaking* and *writing*. In other words, the twofold talent of understanding the written and the spoken language, respectively leads to the arts of writing and speaking, as is the case in the native language. It is by judicious exercises of imitation, founded on the possession of this double talent, that a student will easily acquire the two arts dependent thereon. The repetition of the impressions received by the eye and the ear, fixes the materials of discourse in the mind. *Impression* and *expression* mark the principal subdivision and the order of linguistic studies.

A young child receives his first notions of the national idiom from those who speak to him; an adolescent or an adult who learns a foreign language, which he does not hear habitually spoken, is unable to follow the identical process of nature, and adopts one perfectly analogous, which reason prescribes: he has recourse to books, as a means of initiation in that language. To read a book is to listen to its author, it is learning a language by practice and imitation, no less than is done by a child who hears it spoken. There is a complete analogy between these two modes of proceeding; translation interprets the foreign idiom, as the language of action interprets the national idiom.

Books, as models of expression, are preferable to conversation. They exhibit more especially the right usage, the only guide for speaking and writing in conformity with the genius of a language. Not only do they present a richer stock of words, and a style generally more correct and less trivial than that of conversation, but the impressions made through the organ of sight are more vivid and more lasting than those which are made through the organ of hearing; for the attention is more fully commanded by the eyes than by the ears. This observation applies to the form of language, not to the thought, which, by the force of sympathy, receives from the living voice and the looks of the speaker a power of impressiveness, of which the inert page is altogether destitute.

*Reading*, as an initiation to the knowledge of a language, has a decided advantage over *hearing*.* We have a greater command over what we read than over what we hear. In reading we can pause at will, and direct attention to the passages which require investigation; we can compare what strikes us at the moment, with what precedes, and thus the whole is better connected in the mind and more thoroughly understood.

In listening, on the contrary, the slowness of our conception, or the volubility of the speaker, does not always permit us to follow him. We have not time to dwell on the words or phrases which call for explanation, and much less can we

* The word *hearing* commonly means the act of the ear which perceives the sounds; but we attach to it the idea of comprehending the spoken language. The division of our subject and the absence of a special term, justify the second application given here to this word, by analogy with those which designate the three other arts. *Speaking*, its counterpart, signifies the act both of uttering articulate sounds and expressing ideas. *Reading* means both to pronounce the written words and conceive the ideas conveyed by them. *Writing* applies equally to the manual art of penmanship and to the expression of thought. The mental operation expressed by the second acceptation of these words is the meaning attached to them throughout this essay.

trace back our steps, in order to compare the different parts of the subject and judge of the whole. The rapidity with which most people utter their words in ordinary conversation, requires them to be frequently repeated in order to be retained, whereas, by dwelling as long as we please on written words, we always have it in our power to make sure of them as we proceed in reading. The progress made in learning a language must be at once more certain and more rapid by reading than by hearing.

In the mother tongue a child naturally acquires the pronunciation subsequently to the meaning of words, and remains ignorant of the written signs, which he is afterward taught by a special process, based on his knowledge of the articulate words; he passes from the ideas to the sounds, and from the sounds to the letters. The spoken language, the direct sign of his ideas, gives him the key to the written language.

In the same manner, but in an inverse order, he who learns a language from books becomes acquainted, in the first instance, with the written expression, which is for him, as for the deaf and dumb, the direct sign of thought, and will afterward, by ear-practice, learn the pronunciation corresponding to the written words with which he is familiar. The more perfect his comprehension of the written language, the more rapid will be his progress in the spoken language.

When words have been long observed in books, and heard from the teacher's lips, associated with the ideas they represent, no difficulty will be experienced in reproducing their orthography and pronunciation, the preliminary acquisitions for writing and speaking. The first two arts, considered also as ultimate objects, again claim priority over these, as being, through life, far more useful.

This order is the more rational, as it is much easier to hear or read a language than to speak or write it. The first two arts require of the learner only a slight acquaintance with the words and phraseology; and, in many cases, their meaning is apprehended from the context.

In speaking and writing, on the contrary, neither the most acute sagacity nor the greatest inventive power will avail; not only must we previously know the words expressive of the ideas to be conveyed, but we must also be intimately acquainted with their various shades of meaning, their orthography and pronunciation, their inflections, and syntactic or idiomatic arrangements.

Among the eager crowds who press around a great orator, or among the thousands who read a good author, how few there are, who could speak like the one or write like the other! In fact, a very limited education will suffice for the complete mastery of the arts of hearing and reading; but to write and speak well are the fruit of long study, and the exclusive privilege of superior intelligence and extensive information. The longest life would not suffice to attain perfection in the last two arts, even in the national idiom.

In point of usefulness, writing a foreign language comes last, and reason suggests that what is least needed should be last learned; we must, therefore, as in the vernacular, place speaking before writing, which is only its representative—the thing signified before the sign.

On the other hand, conversation is not attended with the same inconvenience, nor is there the same necessity for precision as in epistolary correspondence, or any other kind of composition. Errors in speaking may always be corrected at the time they are committed. A learner is able to converse much sooner than to write a letter; because oral expression, aided by the language of action, requires fewer words than written composition, which is deprived of this auxiliary. The interchange of ideas in conversation presents more inducements than the elaborate task of epistolary composition, and affords greater facilities for acquiring the phraseology of the teacher by imitation and analogy.

Let it be well understood that this order, on which we insist in the progressive course of studies, does not mean that the learner must be completely master of each of these arts before proceeding to the next; but that he ought, at the outset, to direct his attention exclusively to the first object, then divide it successively between that and the other three, as his progress in each makes it an aid to the acquisition of the others. These different objects having become familiar, may be studied together, without any risk of confusion.

Such is the nature of the human mind: it embraces a diversity of known objects without confounding them; but two new ones create perplexity, when considered simultaneously. Neither will be known, if not studied separately. "Divide and conquer," a political maxim of Machiavelli, applies equally to instruction.

The order to be followed in the study of a foreign language is, therefore, as follows:

1. The art of reading.
2. The art of hearing.
3. The art of speaking.
4. The art of writing.

In the first two arts the words recall the ideas; in the last two the ideas suggest the words.

The direct association of the ideas with their signs is what constitutes the real practical knowledge of a language, and what, in course of time, forms habits which make it the instrument of thought. This end is attained by a system of judicious repetitions. Repetition is indeed the soul of a good method; it engenders habit, and habit fixes the acquirements in the memory.

Perfectible and communicative as we are, Divine Providence has endowed us with two great instincts which, by continually impelling us toward our destiny, create that habit and insure success in the acquisition of language. These are *curiosity* and *imitation*. Curiosity, that noble privilege of humanity, that insatiable desire to know, is ever on the lookout for new sensations, for new ideas, and thus enriches the mind: it is the source of progress in the arts of *reading* and *hearing*. Imitation, the basis of education, identifies us with our fellow-men, and prompts us to adopt their language with their notions, in order to communicate our thoughts to them: it is the source of progress in the arts of *speaking* and *writing*.

In his mother tongue, a child, whether he listens or speaks, practices the association of ideas with their signs unconsciously, by the mere impulse of nature. But, when a second language is studied through the first, it is by comparing one with the other—in other words, by translation—that the learner passes from the known to the unknown, and attaches ideas to the foreign expression; some effort and a firm determination are then required to adopt the direct association of ideas with words.

The first process is the *natural* or *practical* method; the second, the *artificial* or *comparative* method. The latter cannot of itself insure the perfect knowledge of a language; but, as it calls for reflection and judgment, it becomes a useful auxiliary for the development of the intellect.

The practical knowledge of a foreign living language requires the successive application of these two methods; for it must have been interpreted for some time by the native idiom, before its words can be associated directly with the ideas. This double process is the *practical-comparative* method, which is chiefly the subject of this essay.

All extraneous exercises not tending directly to that knowledge, are only accessories more or less useless, or rather impediments placed in the way of youth by blind routine.

The period of learning will be shortened, if the method be sparing of those preparatory exercises, which sacrifice the end for the means, and which not only render the student's labor unprofitable, should he discontinue the pursuit, but also divest study of interest, by keeping out of sight the object at which he aims. The special exercises to which recourse is had for acquiring an art, should always be identified with the art itself, and be its practical application.

The young child, left to himself, rejects theories, and at once avails himself of all the new acquisitions he makes in his own language; nothing prevents learners from following this example in another. If, in the task imposed on them, they see something which is really useful to be gained, and constantly in prospect, they will be stimulated by the thought that their efforts must have a practical result. Being able to apply the knowledge acquired, as they advance, success becomes for them a powerful incentive, and a continual source of enjoyment. Thus, a good method makes the path of duty one of pleasure.

The great secret in education consists in exciting and directing the will: that system is the best which elicits the greatest amount of voluntary exertion from the learner. By calling forth all the resources of the student, and making him conscious of his progress, a rational method leads him to incessant spontaneous efforts; it does not dispense with labor, it directs and seconds it; it does not impose learning on the memory, it indicates the means of acquiring it, of making discoveries, and thus renders study accessible to those who are unable to procure masters.

The prevailing notion that we must be taught every thing is a great evil. The most extensive education, given by the most skilful masters, often produces but inferior characters; that alone which we give to ourselves elevates us above mediocrity. The eminence attained by great men is always the result of self-imposed labor.

On the other hand, exclusive dependence on a professor might prove fallacious in the present state of educational science, when teaching is purely empirical; those who select it for a profession do not usually prepare for it by pedagogical studies; and, in their inexperience, they do not always succeed in imparting to their pupils the knowledge which they possess. To know *what* to teach and *how* to teach are two very different things. This is more especially the case with the teaching of living languages, a career mostly entered upon accidentally by those who, from unfavorable circumstances, have not the choice of a better one.

He who feels the want of learning a language, and who, having a definite object in view, is determined to attain it, will always rely on his own efforts, rather than on the ability or knowledge of a professor. With a view to direct the unaided efforts of students, we have marked out the task which devolves on them. The professor, on his part, must encourage their spontaneousness, and teach them only what they cannot learn by themselves.

The better to effect this object, the exercises we recommend are chiefly those which, by presenting good models to the learners, guard them against errors, that only serve to render indispensable the aid of an instructor, and are a bar against good habits: these are formed by the practice of what is right, not by the correction of what is wrong.

With regard to children as yet incapable of self-direction, they must be assisted through the whole course of their studies. But the younger they are the slower will be their progress. It is a strange mistake to think, as many people do, that the great facility with which children acquire their own language is a proof of their aptitude for learning languages in general, and that this study suits them best.

It is not, as commonly believed, because memory predominates in a child, that he masters his language so easily. This acquirement does not consist in learning words: his attention is engaged with complete propositions, not with individual words; and yet he firmly retains the latter, in consequence of their frequent recurrence and their association with the ideas on which his mind is bent. The admirable spirit of inquiry which Nature has given to the child, is soon checked, if we present to him words instead of the ideas he wants.

His progress is the consequence of his physical and natural condition, which makes his native tongue an object of incessant attention; he does not receive an idea nor experience any sensation, pleasure, or pain, that is not accompanied by an expression, which is thus engraved on his memory by association.

The practical method, by which we learn our native idiom, requires only the instinctive exercise of curiosity, which calls forth the action of the perceptive and imitative faculties. The comparative method, which leads to the knowledge of a language through the medium of another, requires, on the contrary, the coöperation of intellectual powers far greater than are possessed by young children.

It is only when the student can command attention and concentrate it on the objects of study, when he can call to his aid reflection and judgment, when the maturity of his reason enables him to comprehend serious books; it is then and only then that he can study by himself, and learn a second language through his own. The better he knows the latter, the more easily will he learn the former.

Under the conviction of this truth, and with a view to laying a proper foundation for the comparative study of foreign languages, we have dwelt at some length on the course of instruction by which an extensive practical knowledge of the native idiom may be gained during the first period of youth.*

From his earliest years, it is true, the child shows a wonderful aptitude for learning languages; but it is exclusively by practice. The constant need, which, from his helpless condition, the child has of those who surround him, and his anxiety to know their thoughts, and enter into communication with them, make it necessary for him to seize on the great bond of union that connects him with his fellow-creatures. Thus has the Supreme Being endowed us in early infancy with the inclinations and faculties which gratify this first yearning after social life.

If an infant be spoken to in a foreign as frequently as in his native tongue, he will become equally familiar with both. He might, in this

* See book iv. of "Language as a Means of Mental Culture," etc.

way, solely guided by nature, learn from the cradle two or three languages without confounding them, if brought into daily contact with persons who spoke them in his presence, as is frequently the case in the higher classes of society, in which children learn the use of several languages. They have governesses and servants of different countries, who always address them each in his own language.

Every period of life has its special obligations and occupations which prepare for the next. We must not anticipate the course of nature, and require of one period what belongs to another. Before the age of twelve or thirteen, a child cannot learn a language from books by the aid of his own; the weakness of his understanding, his want of motives for study, and his reluctance for sedentary occupations, thwart the efforts of the master, who then employs more time in ascertaining whether his pupils have clearly understood him, and have learned their lessons, than he devotes to real teaching. This observation applies more particularly to classical studies; they are commenced too soon and commenced the wrong way. It cannot even be said, in favor of the early study of a foreign idiom, that it makes a deeper impression on the mind; out of a hundred persons who have studied a language by the comparative method before their twelfth year, ninety-nine have but a faint recollection of it a few years after they have left school.

The incomplete knowledge which a young child possesses either of things or of his own language is, as well as the immaturity of his intellect, an impediment to his comprehending foreign authors. He must indeed find it difficult to render the noble thoughts and admirable style of great writers, when, as yet, he has conceived only the simplest ideas, and has at his command only the most familiar expressions.

With the help of a dictionary, he may translate every word of a foreign author; but, in many cases, he will still remain ignorant of his meaning; because a dictionary in two languages gives the corresponding terms without defining them, or explaining their signification. The child does no more than render one unknown word by another equally unknown—a baneful practice, which accustoms him to take sound for sense, and disposes him, for the rest of his life, to indulge in empty talk and false reasoning.

But, should even a child succeed, with his

master's assistance, in rendering the original text with tolerable accuracy, this is not the true end to be attained. It is degrading great writers, ancient or modern, to subject them to a translation which gives the letter, not the spirit, of the original, and to make their noble pages mere parsing-lessons. They are entitled to a more honorable rank. The scope of their works, the wisdom of their views, and the beauty of their diction, ought to be not only appreciated, but imitated in the national language, a task far beyond the powers of childhood.

The important lessons to be learned, and the intellectual enjoyments to be derived from ancient literature, are lost to the mature man, owing to the childish conceptions which he associated with the classics at school, and to the unpleasant recollection of all the misery attendant on the study. "The flowers of classic genius with which the teacher's solitary fancy is most gratified," says Sir Walter Scott, "have been rendered degraded in his imagination, with tears, with errors, and with punishments; so that the Eclogues of Virgil and the Odes of Horace are each inseparably allied in association with the sullen figure and monotonous recitation of some blubbering schoolboy." Such are the pernicious consequences of the premature study of the classics, that Lord Byron, whose mind was so well fitted to enjoy the beauties of Horace, had he read his writings at the proper time, complains in poetical and bitter strains of the unconquerable dislike with which the scholastic system had inspired him for that poet.

Lamartine makes an observation of the same tendency, in his "Pilgrimage to the Holy Land." "Each wave," he says, "brings me nearer to Greece. I touch its soil; its appearance affects me deeply, much less, however, than it would have done if all these recollections were not accompanied by the consciousness that instruction was forced on me to satiety and disgust before I could comprehend it. Greece is to me like a book of which the beauties are tarnished, because I was compelled to read it before I could understand it. . . . . . I prefer a tree, a spring under a rock, an oleander on the banks of a river, or the fallen arch of a bridge, covered with the foliage of some climbing evergreen, to the monuments of one of these classic kingdoms, which recall to my mind nothing but the ennui they gave me in my boyhood."

In order to give a more distinct idea of the principles propounded in the preceding pages, we will recapitulate them in the following maxims, which may be considered as the axioms of our method:

1. Nature is our best guide in the study of languages.

2. To think in a language is the primary condition for knowing it.

3. The study of the signs implies the previous possession of the ideas.

4. The association of ideas with their signs results from practice.

5. To practise a language is to receive and express ideas through it.

6. Curiosity and imitation are the source of progress in the study of languages; hence,

(1.) Example is better than precept;

(2.) Practice should precede theory.

7. We must, following the dictates of nature, proceed from the whole to its parts.

8. The means should be consistent with the end.

9. We should never lose sight of the end proposed.

10. What we wish to remember must be converted into a habit.

11. One thing only should be done at a time, and every thing in its time.

12. Reading leads to hearing, hearing to speaking, and speaking to writing.

# CHAPTER II.

## THE ART OF READING.

"Lire, lire, et toujours lire dans la langue étrangère, c'est le moyen par excellence."

AJASSON DE GRANSAGNE.

To read is to conform to one of the laws of our nature—the instinct of curiosity; it is to follow on the page the ideas which the writer has consigned to it; it is to appropriate them, as well as the forms under which he presents them.

Books, the depositories of the intellectual treasures which generations bequeath to succeeding generations, are the most efficient instruments of instruction in all the branches of literature and science. The variety of information which a proper course of reading brings under the consideration of a student, and the opportunities it affords him of surmounting the intricacies presented by the different acceptations of words, by technical expressions, and idiomatic forms, will secure the means of enjoying the commerce of the well informed and taking part in their conversation.

The nations with which foreign languages enable us to exchange thoughts, having diverse origins, living under different climates, brought up in habits and subject to laws peculiar to themselves, must also have ideas and opinions differing from ours. Their writers must see in a different light many questions which have also been treated by our national authors. In history, in politics, in belles-lettres, in the arts, and in other departments of knowledge, their notions often widely differ from ours; the perusal of their works will therefore enlarge the circle of our ideas and bring us nearer to the truth.

In short, the habitual reading of good works in different languages has a most beneficial influence on our understanding; it stores the memory with knowledge, and leads, by the force of sympathy and imitation, to the highest conceptions, and to the practice of all that is great and good. By continual contact with superior minds, we not only come to feel their emotions, to think their thoughts, and to speak their language, but our own sentiments are refined, our thoughts elevated, and our power of expression extended.

A good book is the best companion of our leisure hours; we can at any time have recourse to it, and select one from which, as we feel inclined, we may derive either amusement or instruction. It is otherwise with men; we cannot command their services for either purpose, when we are inclined to converse, and it rarely happens that our thirst after knowledge can be satisfied by those we meet in society.

We have not here to treat of reading considered as the art of attaching to the written words the articulate sounds, which they represent, and which, in the mother tongue, recall to the mind their correlative ideas; this is not the case in a language of which we do not know the pronunciation, nor can the written words lead to it; because the sign recalls the thing signified only to one who knows that thing, the art of reading the native, and that of reading a foreign language, cannot be assimilated.

The art of reading, which, in the case of a foreign language, is the most useful, both as an end and as a means, may be acquired without the assistance of a master. If, in infancy, we learn, alone, to understand the spoken language, and afterward to speak it, we ought to be able, in the maturity of reason, to learn, unaided, how to understand the written language and write it.

To teach one's self how to read a foreign language is almost a necessity; for it often happens that a foreigner who teaches his own language is not sufficiently versed in that of his pupils to explain the text of authors, to indicate the expressions equivalent to those of the original, or to correct the mistakes they make in translating.

It is by no means a rare occurrence, that a person, unable to earn a living in his own country, goes abroad with the intention of teaching his native language, without previously preparing himself by learning that of the country where he wishes to establish himself as a teacher, and without even thoroughly knowing his own. Goldsmith, the author of the "Vicar of Wakefield," relates how he went to Holland with a view to teaching English there, but found, on his arrival, that a knowledge of the Dutch language, of which he was utterly ignorant, was indispensable for the realization of his project. He then thought that the wisest course he could take was to return to England by the very same ship which had brought him thence.

An unknown text can be explained only by a

known text, which is its equivalent, and which cannot be discovered by one ignorant of the language, for we can translate only what we understand. This equivalent, or translation, a professor must know perfectly, in order to present it *viva voce* to his pupils when very young. A printed translation will suffice for students who are old enough to dispense with a master.

Grammar affords no assistance in reading; it does not explain the meaning of phrases or words, which is the only difficulty encountered in learning to read a foreign language. The translation which interprets the unknown text, not the grammatical condition of the words, must be the first, the only object for the beginner's consideration. Grammar may teach a person who speaks or writes incorrectly, how to speak or write correctly, but it certainly is not the *art of reading and understanding a language.* No one has ever been insane enough to attach to it this definition. This twofold acquisition is, as we have clearly shown, the first thing to be mastered by students: grammar, therefore, is obviously useless at the entrance on the study.

Syntax, more especially, cannot be an auxiliary, inasmuch as, contrary to the order of nature, it puts precept before example, theory before practice, and makes us pass from words to their combinations. In the progressive development of the intellect, the perception of an object always precedes the consideration of its parts; we learn to understand our own language by passing from the phraseology to the words. The latter have no value but that which is assigned to them by the phrase. The function they perform in speech determines the class to which they belong, as well as their signification. Resorting to the phrase for an explanation of the words is to proceed from the idea to the sign.

If we then wish to follow the prescriptions of nature in acquiring the art of reading a foreign language, we must not prepare for it by learning either its grammar or its words. The latter can be known only in books, by means of the context which fixes their signification. It is not by a previous study of words that we come to understand what is said to us in our own tongue; on the contrary, it is by hearing and reading that we form a vocabulary for ourselves. "Is not," says De Gérando, "the nomenclature of a language, taught as a preparatory exercise, whatever care may be taken, most uninteresting, and hence most prejudicial to the first stage of the study, when it is so important to make this first stage easy and attractive?"

He will, however, make an exception in favor of a very limited class of words.

The elements of speech which form what we call the first class of words, are the *substantives*, *adjectives*, and *verbs*. They are significant by themselves, and constitute the essential parts of a proposition.

The other elements of speech, forming the second class, the *articles*, *pronouns*, *prepositions*, *adverbs*, and *conjunctions*, merely serve to connect, modify, and complete the sense of the other three species of words.*

* We do not include *interjections* in our classification; because, different from the other elements of speech, they are not conventional terms, and have not any fixed character; they vary in their pronunciation and application with the temperament of individuals, and the different emotions which give them birth. As instinctive cries of nature, they are universal, and belong to the language of action, not to any particular idiom. It is then an error to class these inarticulate sounds among the parts of speech, especially as they never enter into the construction of sentences, and are not subject to any syntactical law. Laughter, shrieks, and all other involuntary vocal convulsions, might as justly be called parts of speech.

These remarks apply to interjections properly so called, not to

To these words we will add the *expletives*, which have been denied a place in grammatical nomenclature, although acting an important part in discourse. They serve to point out the grammatical condition or function of the words before which they are placed, such as *to*, the sign of the present of the infinitive mood, and *shall*, the sign of the future. *Il* (it) in French, is an expletive, when it marks the impersonality of the verb.

It is to the second class of words that the above-mentioned exception refers. An acquaintance with them might be useful, if gained at the outset, or studied simultaneously with the practice in reading; for, although apparently of secondary importance, they are the binding links of discourse, and materially modify the sense of sentences.

Committing to memory words of the first class would not assist a beginner; for as their different acceptations depend on a phraseology as yet unknown, the vagueness of their import in a vocabulary would occasion difficulties. But, besides these different acceptations, their other essential

exclamatory expressions, such as, away! bravo! heaven! hark! help! murder, etc., which, although ranked among interjections, are elliptical propositions, formed from different classes of words.

elements, pronunciation, orthography, inflections, syntactical concord, and place in the sentence, constitute a series of considerations which the attention could not embrace at the entrance upon the study.

The absence of connection between these words in vocabularies must also make it difficult to retain them. Even if they were remembered, they would be of little avail in translating; for different subjects, different styles having terms peculiar to each, and rarely to be met with in works to which they do not properly belong, the student might not meet in his first volume with many of those which he had been at so much pains to learn. It is from the connected discourse in which they are incorporated, that their precise import can be ascertained. In imitation, therefore, of what occurs in acquiring the vernacular, these words must, in the foreign tongue, be learned, by reading and hearing, and not be made the means of learning these branches.

The words of the second class, on the contrary, enter into all compositions, whatever be the subject or the style; most of them having only one signification, acquaintance with it will facilitate the understanding of the text. The uniformity of their orthography, and their very limited number (not 400), will render their acquisition easy; while their frequent recurrence in every thing the student reads, will fix them firmly in his memory. Let any one open a French duodecimo volume, and he will find that every line contains four, five, or more words of this class. In number they form a hundredth part of the other words; but, in composition, they occur twice as often; so that each word of the second class is used on an average two hundred times oftener than one of the first class.

A previous acquaintance with these words will prove useful, especially in reading French; because, as their orthography differs completely from that of the corresponding terms in English, their meaning cannot be divined like that of substantives, adjectives, and verbs, three-fourths of which bear great resemblance to each other in the two languages.

As the means should always be consistent with the end, it will suffice to study their form, so as to be able to recognize them at sight. The same may be done with the inflections of the verbs, and those of substantives in languages which admit of cases. This is not learning grammar: the words of the second class, the declensions and conjugations, considered apart from any technological distinction or syntactical functions, but only as regards the ideas they express, appertain to lexicology, not to grammar. However, in the absence of a special collection of them, they may be found in their respective places in all the grammars which give the classification of the parts of speech.

At this early period of the study, and for the object now in view, it would be worse than useless to commit these words to memory, as the student would thereby infallibly acquire a bad pronunciation. Out of fifty syllables formed of the same letters in French and in English, there is scarcely one which represents exactly the same sound in both languages; so that, in pronouncing French words, which he has never heard, the learner is likely to be wrong forty-nine times out of fifty.

If, however, owing to the habit of always pronouncing in his own language the words which he sees, he cannot help doing the same with those of another language, he must, when ignorant of its pronunciation, be content to give mentally to the letters of the foreign words the sound which they have in his own language: this will be, as it were, a mere spelling, not an attempt at pronunciation. The vocal organs, remaining, in the mean while, quiescent, will not contract any habit which must be got rid of afterward.

*Direct reading*, that by which the written expression, as in the native idiom, directly conveys the thought, is the end to be attained. *Indirect reading*, that by which the idea is apprehended through the medium of the mother-tongue, that is, *translation*, is only an introduction to direct reading. At an advanced stage of the study, translation becomes an obstacle to the understanding of the language, for it is not always possible. So would spelling, which is an auxiliary in learning to read one's own language, prove an obstacle to reading if persevered in.

The process by which a learner is enabled to follow directly the train of an author's ideas cannot be made too easy. This spontaneous association of the ideas with the words that represent them constitutes the real practice of the foreign language, and the groundwork on which advancement in all its other departments is based. Translation, on the contrary, being the practice of the national idiom, becomes thereby a most efficient means of improvement in it.

But, as direct reading can be arrived at only through the medium of translation, the student must, as a preliminary step toward it, attend seriously to the latter. No parsing, no grammatical comment on the language: all he requires is to advance rapidly in the comprehension of the text in hand, that he may become acquainted with a large number of words and phrases. Practice is now the object; we will subsequently suggest modes of mental culture.

The first books to be used should treat of familiar subjects, and be written in an easy style, in order to avoid encountering at the same time the difficulty of the subject and that of the language. Attention is then directed to the form, not to the matter; it is absorbed in the work of translation. All serious instruction, apart from the language itself, would be ill-timed.

These books are, as it were, only practical or reading vocabularies, but vocabularies addressed to the understanding as well as to the memory, and the words of which have a definite meaning. They will familiarize the student with the terms and phraseology of ordinary conversation, at the same time that they will lay the foundation for studies of a higher character. The elements of discourse, by the daily practice of reading, like all daily occurrences, remain in the memory without effort, as deposits from the stream of experience.

Correctness of language is nearly all that is required in the text of these initiatory books. Any other merit would be lost, at least out of place, at a period when it cannot possibly be distinguished, still less appreciated, especially as the meaning is reached only by translation.

The initiatory texts to be translated should be rather below than above the age of the learners, who should never be required to read works which would be above their comprehension if written in the national idiom. In the study of languages, as in that of the fine arts, masterpieces are not fit for beginners; novices always work on materials of an inferior kind. The most eminent writers and orators have, in childhood, passed through the ordeal of trivial language and commonplace ideas.

We insist on this point, because the prevalent notion that none but works written in the most elegant or classical style ought to be put into the hands of beginners, creates the necessity of resorting to various preparatory exercises, and is in opposition to the principle of gradation dictated by nature: it is one of the chief causes both of the discouragement experienced by learners at their entrance upon the study, and of the unreasonable duration of linguistic instruction.

Modern literatures present inexhaustible food to curiosity, and great facilities for the strict application of the principle of gradation of difficulties; they abound in books which, being intended for young people, may serve as an introduction to reading, and as models for learning to speak and write. In this respect, living languages have a great advantage over the dead: in the latter, the number of works which have been handed down to us is too limited to permit in all cases the difficulty of the task to be adapted to the learner's capacity. Their elevated character is beyond the reach of immature minds; it is therefore the understanding of the learner which, by proper delay, must be raised to the standard of the classics. What is above the capacity of a boy of ten or twelve may have some chance of being understood by a lad of fifteen or sixteen.

The learner must read a considerable quantity of prose before he enters on poetry. It is by gradual steps that, in the native tongue, we are enabled to commune with superior minds. It is absurd to make poetical compositions of a high order a means of study; they are its end, its reward. He who uses them as a means, will not feel a wish to read them when he has learned the language. What shall we say of the common practice of putting into the hands of young people who have read only a few volumes, the works of Dante or of Milton, poets whom their own countrymen can scarcely understand?*

Nor are voluminous works fit for beginners; they lose all their interest, on account of the slowness with which they are read. The kind which appears to combine the most favorable conditions are first the books which treat of subjects familiar to the student, then fables, anecdotes, tales, narratives, and historical sketches; these are subjects of general interest, and become more interesting still if they relate to the nation whose language

* "Chi oramai in Italia, chi è che veramente legga, e intenda, e gusti, e vivamente senta Dante e Petrarca? Uno in mille a dir molto."—ALFIERI.

The style of Milton's "Paradise Lost" had become so antiquated, so obscure, about a hundred years ago, that a bookseller, named Osborne, thought proper to publish a prose version of it for the benefit of "ordinary readers."

is studied. A style intelligible to children and purely narrative, as being the easiest, is the most suitable for beginners, even those of mature intellect. Learners, whatever be their age, will apply the more willingly to this task, as it gratifies instinctive inquisitiveness, and is the least painful of all that are imposed by the study of a language. By facilitating their first steps in reading we command their attention, give them a taste for reading, and secure their success.

The reading of the foreign text may be commenced at the outset, without any preparatory studies or exercises, by means of a literal translation. With the interpretation of that text before his eyes, the student, having first perused an English phrase, will then utter it with his eyes directed to its foreign equivalent; that is, he will translate the latter in mentally attaching, as far as it is practicable, the known to the unknown words. For greater facility in passing from one text to the other, these should be placed opposite to each other in the first books which he uses.

In all countries possessing a literature, the best works have been translated and are daily translated from one language into another. There can be no difficulty in procuring these auxiliaries, but, out of the great number of translations, students must select those which, as they render faithfully the foreign text, most closely follow its construction. Their great merit for a beginner is to be literal, and yet written in a clear and correct style. The previous knowledge of the words of the second class and of the inflections of those of the first, which we recommend above, will be the more useful according as the auxiliary translation is less literal.

The mode of interpretation which we recommend is peculiar in so far as it permits a foreign language to be studied through an English translation, or an English original text which has been translated into that language. The same book may, therefore, serve for students of the two countries. All the works, for instance, published in France and in England or America with the French and the English opposite each other, are equally useful to the English or Americans who learn French and to the French who learn English. These interpretations, by removing uncertainty as regards the true meaning of the foreign text, far surpass in efficiency the usual mode of translating with the help of a dictionary, which continually leads to errors that call for assistance.

They dispense with the necessity of either a master or a dictionary. The enormous time consumed by the latter, and the perplexity arising from its various interpretations, discourage beginners, and delay their progress, when they have to look out for nearly all the words of their author.

Words, moreover, which are thus translated one by one, present but a vague meaning, and frequently none, to a child as yet little versed in his own language. Their signification depends on the very text the sense of which he is seeking. To find out the unknown through the unknown, such is the circle in which he is placed by the dictionary.

It is partly owing to this illogical, repulsive, and unnatural process that must be attributed, for the great majority of young persons, the signal failure of linguistic studies. With the aid of a dictionary they hardly translate, and translate badly, twenty-five or thirty lines a day, about a volume in the course of a year, whereas twenty-five or thirty volumes at least should be read to secure the complete acquisition of the art of reading.

Some people imagine that the use of the dictionary impresses the words on the memory, forgetting that this mode of coming at their meaning is not the fruit of reflection, and does not constitute a discovery, any more than being told it or taking it from a translation: it is a mere reliance on the testimony of others, with the additional uncertainty and confusion arising from various interpretations for the same word. Its inefficiency as a mnemonic auxiliary is proved by experience. The languages learned by drudging at it, are mostly forgotten with amazing rapidity. How could it be otherwise, when the use of thumb and fingers is substituted for the exercise of the intellect? The native words gained without the dictionary are retained with extreme tenacity. In any case, that pretended auxiliary is incompatible with the principle of our nature which leads us to pass from the whole to its parts, from the phrase to the words. The dictionary, however, can be made use of when, at an advanced period of the study, the learner meets with few unknown words, and is able from the context to choose the right meaning from among those given in its columns.

The readiness with which a learner through a translation in juxtaposition, seizes the thought of the author, and the logical sequence of the subject, gives an interest to reading, which it cannot have with the dictionary, as the latter, by directing his attention to each word individually, breaks off the connection between the ideas. If the annexed translation enable the learner to get through the text more easily than he can with the dictionary, he will translate more in a given time, so that the same expressions will present themselves the more frequently, according as they are more useful, and, as in the mother-tongue, will be remembered in proportion to their usefulness. Progress is always in an inverse ratio to the time devoted to translating the first volumes. One hundred pages, for instance, read at the rate of ten pages a day, will advance a learner more than the same number would, if read at the rate of one page a day.

The foreign phraseology to a beginner is a true chaos, in which the eye perceives nothing distinctly: by degrees, the frequent reappearance of the same elements in their appropriate places exhibits their essential characteristics and makes the object of attention gradually clearer. After a while, the light begins to dawn, and they all present themselves in intelligible and harmonious order.

The division of the labor which falls to the share of the master and pupils respectively, is favorable to public teaching, as it allows the latter to advance in reading in proportion to their desire of learning and to the time they can spare for study. The quantity which they may read daily should be regulated, not by what an instructor has leisure to hear in the class, but by the time which they can devote to it in their private studies, and by the facility with which they perform the exercise.

All the members of a class, according to their different degrees of proficiency, may read different works, especially as the professor does not make these a subject of examination for each pupil separately. It is, as will be seen, when he comes to initiate them in the art of hearing that he can judge of their diligence in his absence.

In this way, diligent learners are not kept back in their studies by the indolence or incapacity of some of their school-fellows, as frequently happens in the present state of public teaching, in which the professor imposes the same book and the same task on all, without the least regard to the intellectual inequalities that may exist among them. This mode of reducing the intellects and capabilities of all to the same standard, condemns some to a deplorable inactivity, and others to a task above their strength.

The mode of proceeding at the commencement should be nearly as follows: To devote exclusively to the translation of the first volumes all the time one has for study in the absence of the teacher, to go several times over the same passages for some weeks, to peruse every day the lesson of the day before, and gradually throw off dependence on the translation opposite. As the work becomes easier, more will be translated in a given time, and the learner will soon be able to dispense with auxiliary aids.

He should, however, guard against excess in this respect, against premature attempts at perfection. By dwelling too long on the first pages the task would be made tedious and disagreeable, at the very time when his curiosity needs to be stimulated by variety and novelty. Besides, by such dilatory minuteness, words and phrases of rare occurrence would be apt to occupy time and attention to the exclusion of those which are more immediately required; whereas, by steady progress through the book, he will more frequently meet with those which are the most useful, and his acquisition of them will be consistent with the demands of colloquial intercourse. Besides, we can know the full import of words only by meeting with them in various circumstances. We proceed thus in the native tongue and in all the arts. Long concentration of the mind on one subject, like the division of labor in manufactures, creates habits which impair its power.

Although the ordinary practice of teaching has not hitherto favored the publication of works in two languages, there are, nevertheless, a sufficient number in English and in French to initiate learners of either nation in the art of reading the language of the other. Dialogues and collections of phrases in the two languages might even be used for this purpose in the absence of the books recommended.

When, with the aid of two or three of these works, the student has become familiar with a large portion of the foreign phraseology, if not yet able to dispense altogether with assistance, he may have recourse to books in which the more difficult expressions are explained in notes at the foot of the page. Several works of this kind may be obtained for the French and the English languages.

Interlinear translations—among the advocates

of which may be mentioned the great scholars of Port-Royal, Dumarsais, Beauzée, Radonvilliers, Condillac, D'Alembert, and Locke—certainly render an important service, as auxiliaries in reading; we therefore do not absolutely reject them, especially if they are accompanied by a free translation. But, as they make the words subservient to the meaning of the phrase, in opposition to the principle we have laid down, we prefer interpretation on the page opposite to the foreign text, which explains its phraseology. Interlinear translations, in addition to the confusion for the eye, arising from the jumbling together of the two languages, are a constant cause of perplexity from the difference of their construction, and the more so, when the words, as it often happens, are always translated the same way, whatever be their meaning in the text.

As the student advances in the comprehension of the foreign text, he will naturally notice the words which the phrases have in common, and will the more readily apprehend their precise import, in proportion as they often recur and in different circumstances. Not only the words, but their prefixes and affixes, as well as their inflections, will be explained one by the other.

When, at a later period, having laid aside the initiatory books, he meets with new words, their points of resemblance, to those he already knows, their roots or their terminations, the place they occupy or the circumstance that introduces them, will be so many data to lead him by induction to an inference as to their meaning. Not only would this investigation be favorable to mental discipline, but the information thus gained would be more indelibly impressed on the mind, precisely because it had been discovered by mental efforts.

If, on thus appealing to his judgment, he does not succeed in discovering their import, he can then have recourse to a dictionary; and, in this case, to arrive the sooner at direct reading, we should give the preference to a dictionary, exclusively in the language he is learning, which, as it presents the definitions of the words, is less likely to lead him astray than a dictionary in the two languages, which often presents by translation only an approximative sense.

We gain the knowledge of native words by instinctive analysis. The first sentence we hear conveys to the mind an indistinct notion of the meaning of a word, the second makes this notion somewhat clearer, a third and a fourth render conjecture still more definite, until at length, a last induction removes all doubts as regards the idea to be attached to it. In this manner we come, by almost imperceptible steps, to know the precise meaning of a considerable number of abstract terms, which no definitions could ever make us understand.

Nearly all the words that we know in our own language, have been divined in this manner. This is a mental operation far superior to reliance on a dictionary, which is, after all, a mere mechanical operation. What is discovered by mental effort, is more thoroughly known and better retained than what is learned from a book or from a teacher.

Three months ought to suffice, without any very great labor, to read five or six small volumes, and even to read them twice over. Then, as greater facilities in reading make it a more attractive occupation, the student will read more, and will advance toward perfection with rapid strides.

These results, due to the diligence of self-taught learners, cannot, however, be expected from children whose age requires the aid of a teacher.

Their advancement in reading depends on the time he devotes to them, and will necessarily be slow, especially when, as in public schools, only two or three hours a week are allotted to the teaching of the living languages.

It is incumbent on learners to finish a work once begun; let the instructor recommend none but such as are worthy of being read entirely. Much of the interest and profit is lost, when books are but partially read. The second part of a work generally indemnifies us for the trouble we have had in reading the first. As we advance in a volume we become acquainted with the author's peculiarities of style, and our minds are gradually identified with his. Perseverance in completing the work, necessarily brings a repetition of the same words and phraseology, and thus engraves them in the memory. The comparative facility also with which the latter part is read is a source of pleasure, and a manifest indication of improvement; it is unreasonable to deprive students, as is often done, of this gratification, of this stimulus to further exertion, by making them read only portions of works. More unreasonable still is it to expect that learners can become conversant with the literature of a country by the study of extracts from various authors, however judicious their selection.

The merit of a good book, moreover, does not depend exclusively on minute details of style; it also consists in the end which the author had in view, in the conception of the general plan, and in the harmony of all its parts.

"If a book be worth reading once," says Benjamin Franklin, "it should be read twice." We will add, if, at an advanced stage, it is not worth reading twice, it ought not to be read at all. A second reading is indispensable both for advancing in the art of reading, and for retaining the materials of conversation. It is indeed impossible, on the first reading of a book, to perceive all its force and propriety of expression, or even to attend to the orthography or arrangement of the words, the attention being then engaged by the effort required for understanding the text.

On a second or third perusal, familiarity with the matter and the rapid association of expressions and ideas, enable the reader to divide his attention and bestow part of it on the composition of words, their fitness, and their arrangement. Some read much, who yet write very incorrectly; because they attend exclusively to the subject, and never bestow a thought on the form of language. If the course we suggest be adopted, orthography, in particular, will present no difficulty; the frequent recurrence of the same words in reading will render the eye an instinctive judge in spelling, as is the educated ear in pronunciation.

The impressions which are made by the first acquaintance with standard works are usually confused; it is only on closer acquaintance with them that the mind acquires the power of perceiving the connection of the parts, the character of the whole, the suitableness of the style to the thoughts, and all the beauties of composition, as well as the inaccuracies which have escaped the author. The repeated perusal of a work furnishes the surest means by which its literary merit can be tested; for productions of sterling worth afford new pleasures, and unfold new beauties at each successive reading, whilst those of inferior character scarcely bear a second perusal; they exhibit more imperfections, according as they are more frequently or attentively read.

If a person, when reading alone, meets with passages he does not clearly understand, and cannot, at the moment, obtain the explanations he needs, let him mark them with pencil in the margin, he will generally find that all the difficulties disappear on a second reading of the volume: such is the fruit of practice.

Repetition is the grand principle on which depends the efficacy of the processes required for gaining a practical knowledge of a language. To impart to the intellectual powers a certain freedom of action, repetition is as necessary as exercise to the limbs. Six months of continuous application will lead to greater proficiency than twelve months of lessons with frequent interruptions. Habits of language can be created only by keeping the same words and phrases in rapid succession before the mind: the same number of impressions which, when closely following each other, produce a habit, would fail to do so, if separated by long intervals.

The reading of the great writers should be deferred until it can be effected without the medium of a translation. It is only by direct reading that the mind, free from considerations apart from the subject, can enter fully into the author's meaning. Neither scientific nor philosophical works can be studied with the same advantage by translating as by direct reading. A search after the native expressions corresponding to those of the original breaks in constantly upon the connection of the subject; and the mind, thus diverted, cannot easily follow a train of close reasoning.

The qualities of style which constitute the chief merit of works of imagination are entirely lost by an extempore translation in which the form is necessarily neglected for the substance, the mind being exclusively engaged in rendering the identical ideas of the foreign text; poetry, especially, cannot be read through translation. All that constitutes its beauty, its charm, disappears in passing into another language.

No two languages correspond word for word, phrase for phrase: they all differ in their genius. Each has numerous expressions without equivalents in another, and consequently ideas which cannot be exactly represented in the latter. Hence, the scarcity of faithful translations. There is some truth in the Italian proverb, "Traduttore traditore." "Next to a good tragedy," says Voltaire, "nothing is more difficult to write than a good translation." "Of all books," says also Lamartine, "the most difficult to be written is, in my opinion, a translation."

The best of them, those which are made by eminent writers, and meditated in the silence of the closet, are, for the most part, but imperfect copies of the master-pieces which they are intended to represent. What must be the extempore translation of students, who as yet do not know the foreign language, and frequently are only smatterers in their own? When the reading of the foreign language is the only object proposed, it is a waste of time and useless trouble to polish the phraseology corresponding to that of the original text. If the latter is understood, the end is gained. What signifies the manner of expressing the same ideas in a second language? We will even go further; it is not the translation which leads to the exact sense of the foreign text, but the clear understanding of that text, which secures the means of translating it properly.

With regard to irregularities of construction in idiomatic phrases, the student will do well to be satisfied with the interpretation of his text, as given by a good translation. Much must at first be taken for granted, consistently with that vital principle, "practice before theory." Inquiring into the reasons of the peculiarities of a foreign idiom only impedes progress through the book without making it more intelligible. Let the reader reflect that, in his own language, he can seldom solve difficulties of this sort: he could not account for innumerable anomalies and idiomatic forms; although, in common practice, he would properly apply every expression, and would never hesitate about their signification. Few English persons, for example, even among the well-educated, know or care to know the reasons of the following deviations from grammar or from the proper meaning of words: *two dozen; a few salmon; a brace of snipe, of partridge, etc.; many a day; now-a-days; methinks; would I were there now; were I to put up with it; I had rather stay; you had better be off;* and a thousand other equally odd expressions in daily use. The case is just the same with the idioms of other languages.

The chief obstacle which translation opposes to the complete possession of the foreign language, is owing to the fact that, being placed between the foreign expression and the thought, it prevents their direct association, and consequently the instantaneous suggestion of one by the other. To be conscious of a sensation and retain it, the attention must be directed simultaneously, with the action of the organ, on the object of sensation. In translation the foreign text, it is true, is before the eye, but the learner's whole attention is given to the forms of the language into which he translates; the translator thinks in the language in which he has embodied the thought, and so the foreign expression leaves no trace in his mind. This process, the one usually insisted on, engenders a habit which excludes the possibility of thinking in that language and retaining its phraseology. Here we find an additional reason for dispensing with the services of a master in this first stage of the study, since he cannot assist his pupils in understanding a foreign author, save through translation.

The oral translation of several volumes having familiarized the student with a considerable portion of the vocabulary and idiomatic phraseology of the foreign language, he will drop the practice of translating, in order to take in the ideas directly from the author. A few efforts in this direction will rid him altogether of this inefficient process, and enable him to follow the ideas in the text itself—the first step in the art of thinking in the language. It is especially on the second perusal of a book, or of passages of a book, that he must make his début in direct reading, on account of the facilities offered by his knowledge of the text. After a few days' practice he will find that it is far easier to follow the thought of an author directly than to translate.

Until now pronunciation has been set aside, as affording no aid toward the signification of words, the reverse of what happens in the native idiom, which is acquired by the immediate association of the sense with the sound, and in which the written word is intelligible, only inasmuch as it recalls to the reader a known articulate word. Before the foreign words had been frequently heard, bad habits of pronunciation would be contracted, if a student gave utterance to them as he reads. The time given to the practice, if he aimed at a correct enunciation, would be lost for his advancement in the comprehension of books. Signification, not pronunciation, is the first step to be made in the study of a language.

Three things are to be considered in a word, the *written form*, the *articulate sound*, and *the idea;* the written form is the sign of the articulate sound, as the articulate sound is the sign of the idea. Now, the sign cannot be an object of consideration, unless the thing signified be present to the mind; we must, therefore, be thoroughly impressed with the ideas before attending to the articulate sounds which represent them, and must be acquainted with the sounds, before we turn our attention to the letters.

He who is denied the benefit of a teacher's assistance, contents himself with pronouncing in his own language the expressions corresponding to those of the foreign text, and thereby guards against a false pronunciation. But, when familiarized with the sense of the foreign words, the sounds of which he does not know, he wishes to practise direct reading, the surest means of success will be, as he peruses the text, to utter the words mentally in the manner recommended at page 46. The mind thus engaged will be diverted from translation. Defective as is this mental pronunciation, the vocal organs not being engaged in producing it, no bad habit is contracted, and the self-imposed error will rapidly vanish under the reiterated impressions of the true pronunciation, when the circumstances are favorable for acquiring it.

Should the learner have the benefit of a teacher, he will master the pronunciation in time to apply it to direct reading, if, by the exercises which we shall hereafter describe, his progress in that art has kept pace with his advance in the understanding of the written language, When he is master of the pronunciation he will always attach it to the text, and will thus make it the immediate expression of his thought. The pronunciation of the words in a low voice, while the mind attends to the subject, will form the organs to habits that will aid considerably in using correct language afterward.

Direct reading must be diligently practised, in the absence of the professor, throughout the course. It is impossible to become familiar with all the words and the phraseology of a language, in fine, to understand it like one's own, except by the constant and studious reading of good writers in prose and verse on a variety of subjects. Such is the true, the only way of becoming acquainted with the literature of a country and the genius of its language. To know a language, observes the learned orientalist, Sir William Jones, "we must read an infinite number of works written in it."

Of the 50,000 words, or thereabout, comprised in the vocabulary of a modern language, there are at least 20,000 which should be recognizable by the eye and ear, as coming within an extensive practice in reading or hearing, while 10 or 12,000 ought to be known so as to be readily suggested for the expression of thought in all the circumstances of life. It is obvious that this twofold object can be attained only by a course of diversified reading, embracing all the subjects on which we may have occasion to converse in society.

We do not speak here of the exchange of ideas which may take place in the occasional intercourse with foreigners whom chance brings in our way: a few words will suffice for this object. We have considered it our duty to show the way to perfection: every one is at liberty to stop when his object is attained.

In addition to the difficulty of attaining the ready use of so great a number of words, we must not forget that most of them are taken in different acceptations, a fact which imposes a further task on the memory, and renders extensive reading still more necessary. Nothing but long practice can bring under the reader's notice all the idiomatic combinations, all the circumstances which illustrate these changes of meaning. The more extensive and varied the student's reading, the more copious will be his vocabulary, and the better will he understand the words in their various acceptations.

It is in order to gain familiarity with the

idioms especially—a very numerous class of expressions not accessible through rules—that we must have recourse to the extensive reading of popular works in the absence of social intercourse with foreigners.

The memory is enriched by the repetition attending long practice, and the elements of discourse, thus associated with ideas in the mind, constitute the first condition for speaking a language, as well as for entering into the spirit of its writers. The power of this association is such, that he who should practise it with perseverance, especially in his native tongue, by uttering the language of good writers as he reads them, could not fail to possess a rich stock of ideas with a great facility in extempore speaking. There can be little doubt that many good public speakers have been indebted for their success to this mode of self-training.

Considered as the means of fixing the elements of speech in the memory, reading is indisputably efficacious, even in the native idiom; though, in this case, the habit of familiar and sometimes trivial language is an obstacle to the impressions received in reading well-written works. In fact, great precision of expression is only to be attained by the perusal and the imitation of good writers; for, in books alone, do we find the well-chosen terms and the forms which characterize a noble and graceful style. The influence of books is more decidedly felt in a second language; because the expressions of the foreign author are not exposed to the antagonism of others already known; they strike the mind with all the force of first impressions. Even those who learn a language solely with a view to speaking it, ought to read a great deal. In order to be conversant with all the resources of reason and language, we must necessarily seek them in many books.

The practice of reading, by exercising curiosity, multiplies its energy, and people desire to read, in proportion as they have formed the habit of reading. In accordance with this desire they can always procure books, and thus retain the art of reading to the end of a long life; whereas the double talent of speaking and writing a foreign language is very soon lost for want of practice.

The art of reading foreign languages, if generally cultivated throughout the civilized world, would greatly facilitate international relations: every one writing in his own language would then be understood abroad. Diplomatists, scientific men, and merchants, especially, would derive incalculable advantages from this attainment; they would cease to be dependent on interpreters and clerks, who often write so inaccurately as greatly to perplex their correspondents. International communication has, until this time, been much impeded by the extreme difficulty of writing a foreign language. Very seldom could a person be sure of conveying his meaning in it, with as much clearness and precision as in his own; and if he had correspondents in various countries, it is more probable that they could read his language than that he could write their different idioms so as to be perfectly understood.*

* A student might sometimes be impeded in his progress toward perfection in the art of reading, by the difficulty of procuring all the books indispensable to an extensive course. Every obstacle of this kind would be removed, if the professor would collect a small library composed exclusively of good works in the language which he teaches, with and without the interpretation of the text, and furnish them to his pupils for a small quarterly payment; he would thus have the means of directing them in the choice of books best suited for their use.

# CHAPTER III.

## THE ART OF HEARING.

"It is a mistake to believe that study and practice are not as necessary for hearing as for speaking."

PLUTARCH.

THE advantages arising from social intercourse consist more in receiving than in communicating ideas. Hearing is truly the better half of conversation: it is, in every respect, incomparably more useful than speaking. Like reading, it satisfies instinctive inquisitiveness, one of the principles of human perfectibility.

If we perfectly understand what is said, a few words, a monosyllable, even the slightest motion of assent or dissent, will suffice to keep up conversation or transact business. If, on the contrary, we do not clearly comprehend the person who addresses us, all the command of language which we may possess will be unavailable for social intercourse: hence hearing may be useful independently of speaking; whereas speaking is useless without hearing. It is always more profitable and less dangerous to listen than to speak.

Especially when we are in a foreign country for the first time, every thing is matter of curiosity: we have a great deal of local information to gain from its inhabitants, a thousand opportunities of hearing their language, and comparatively very little to say. If a person understands the spoken language of the country which he visits, he is enabled, from the moment of his arrival, not only to enjoy the society of the inhabitants, but also to improve in speaking; for words and entire phrases are easily retained, when the ear distinctly catches and the mind clearly apprehends them. In the absence of this faculty, he remains isolated in the midst of his fellow-men, and even keeps away from their society, in the dread of exhibiting his ignorance. So that he derives neither profit nor pleasure from a residence abroad; and he might be years in the country without being able to speak its language. "He that travelleth in a foreign country," says Lord Bacon, "before he hath some entrance into the language, goeth to school not to travel."

The comprehension of the spoken language, although the most important element of our social relations, and, at the same time, the most natural and most certain means of learning to speak, has, nevertheless, been so far neglected in the teaching of foreign languages, that there is not even a term by which to express it; and, for the purpose of classification, we have been under the necessity of attaching this new acceptation to the words *hearing* and *audition.*

Many persons do not even suspect this power to be an art; for they have no recollection of having ever learned it in their own language, so easy does nature make its acquisition at the entrance into life. The capability to speak implies, in the vernacular language, that of hearing, which, by the force of imitation, gave it birth. This is not the case with languages learned from books.

The difficulty generally experienced in understanding oral expression is not inherent in the nature of the art: a child sixteen or eighteen months old is already a proficient in it, though he would be utterly incapable of improvement in any other department of language. The difficulty may fairly be attributed to the methods of teaching hitherto followed; they leave the organ of hearing in complete inaction; or only exercise it on detached words and phrases. The ear untaught by the teacher's voice, cannot, in the usual rapidity of speech, recognize the foreign words, however familiar they may be to the eye. The learners are exercised in hearing only in conversation, when they begin to speak. This is putting the cart before the horse, since we cannot join in conversation, unless we understand what is said.

This acquisition is further impeded by the learner's not having previously met in his scanty reading with the phraseology of those with whom he comes in contact; while, from his want of practice in hearing the language, he is unable to associate the ideas with the sounds, and is then obliged to translate what he hears, an operation for which the rapidity of speech does not allow time.

The prescriptions of the preceding chapter tend to remove these obstacles. The student who has followed them, and made some advance in the art of reading, will find himself in a favorable position for advancing in the second branch.

If the art of reading can be acquired without a teacher, it is otherwise with hearing and pronouncing, in which no advance can be made without his aid, and especially without his possessing a correct pronunciation and accent. When a child pronounces his own language incorrectly, it is the fault of those around him; when the learner of a foreign language pronounces it badly, it is the fault of his teacher.

The simple and natural method by which the ear is formed to the articulate sounds of the mother tongue, and by which the vocal organs learn to reproduce them, is equally applicable to a foreign language. If strictly and perseveringly followed, it would enable us to seize the meaning of the words, and acquire the foreign pronunciation as easily as our own. That this end is so seldom attained, only proves the fallacy of the methods pursued. We disdain to follow the easy path which nature has marked out, and are punished by fatigue and disappointment.

The nature of the object proposed sufficiently shows the mode of procedure. If, in the absence of the master, the eye is exercised on orthography, in his presence the ear must be exercised on pronunciation: these two organs afford mutual aid to each other. Reading and hearing must be carried on simultaneously.

A passage of a foreign author being selected, at every lesson, by the professor, from what has previously been studied by the learners, he distinctly reads it aloud in short phrases, which they alternately translate without seeing the text, and the length of which is commensurate with their degree of advancement. Then the whole passage is read a second time without interruption, but slowly enough to permit the learner to translate mentally as he proceeds.

Being assisted in these two exercises in hearing by the recollection of the subject, the recent impression of which is still fresh in their minds, the learners will easily recognize the words which are familiar to the eye. They may perhaps, at first, only make guesses; but these, by their recurrence, will soon become real knowledge, as is the case with every thing that is learned by experience.

The association of the spoken with the written words will be rapidly effected, because the elementary sounds are few in number, and, in consequence, recur frequently; moreover, it will take place naturally, and without any of the difficulties attending the illogical process by which the sounds are usually inferred from the letters in teaching the foreign pronunciation.

The professor will avoid reading isolated

words; for their signification, and especially that of homonyms, that is, of words differing in meaning but resembling in sound, can be understood, on being heard, only from the sentences in which they are incorporated.

If, in reading to a class, the passage selected be the last prepared by the least advanced learner, while he translates it chiefly from recollection, his more advanced fellow-students, who may not have read it for some time previously, will also do the same, owing to their greater familiarity with the language. Thus, all the members of the class, whatever be their different degrees of advancement in reading, will derive equal benefit from this exercise.

In this manner the professor always has it in his power to ascertain the diligence of his pupils in that part of the language which devolves on themselves. As he reads to them for translation the passage which they had to read in his absence, he thus examines them in one branch while exercising them in another; for the pronunciation will not suggest the sense to his pupils, unless it recalls to their minds a text previously studied. And when he wishes to ascertain the progress they have made in orthography by due attention to the written form of the foreign text in preparing their lessons, he will stop at the words, which present some difficulty, and will question them on their spelling, accompanying this examination with explanations and rules which will benefit the whole class, however numerous it may be. This will preclude the necessity of dictations and other orthographical exercises, from which no advantage is derived in proportion to the time they consume.

The reading by fragments will be set aside, and the second, or uninterrupted reading, continued for a longer time at each sitting, when the pronunciation, having grown familiar to the hearers, does not call for great efforts on their part, and thus permits them to attend easily to continuous discourse. The professor will then lead his pupils from the known to the unknown, by reading to them what they have not previously seen; then, by a gradually increasing rapidity of utterance, he compels them to associate the idea with the sound, to pass from translation to the direct comprehension of what is said.

The art of following ordinary conversation presents no difficulty to a person able to understand the language on hearing it read; for the words used in the exchange of ideas are generally more familiar than those which are found in books, the periods are shorter, and the same expressions more frequently repeated, while the delivery, more natural, is accompanied by tones, looks, and gestures, which greatly assist the hearer. The mind is kept alive by the ever-varying topics, and relieved by the successive interruptions of colloquial intercourse. The person spoken to is also more attentive, because he feels more interested in what is personally addressed to him. This truth is forcibly illustrated by the well-known fact that, in public assemblies, extemporaneous speeches are much more favorably received than written discourses.

The professor will accustom his pupils to the forms of conversation, by choosing from the passages read to them, the idiomatical expressions in common use, modifying them in the same manner as is done in familiar intercourse. He may also make such additions, retrenchments, substitutions, transpositions, as his fancy suggests, so as to change the ideas without altering the essential character of the idiom.

As regards his readings, he will gradually lengthen them and make them more rapid in proportion as his pupils, becoming more familiar with the pronunciation, shall begin to understand him without translating. These exercises will soon enable them to understand the spoken language directly, if, while seizing the thought it conveys, they repeat it mentally, as it falls from the professor's lips.

In the mean time the professor will, as explained in the following chapter, communicate to them his pronunciation and accent, and the more easily in proportion as he has trained their ears by much reading. At an earlier period, exercises in pronunciation would have been premature: it has no foundation to rest upon, unless the import of the words is perfectly known, to which it is to be attached. How, indeed, can signs be studied, which do not suggest the things signified?

It is a great mistake to imagine that, in the study of a living language, the pronunciation should be taught first. It does not in any way facilitate the understanding of the written words; and, besides, a person may perfectly understand what he hears, without being able to pronounce correctly. In infancy we know the meaning of words, long before we can utter them. In learning a foreign language we ought also to understand the spoken words before attempting to articulate them.

To study simultaneously both the pronunciation and the signification of words at the beginning is incompatible with that law of our mental organization, which forbids attention to be directed at the same time to several distinct things when new.

In the course of the exercises in audition, the learners should forbear looking at what is read to them, that the ideas may be exclusively received through the articulate words, as when listening to a speaker. If a person familiar with the written language had his eyes fixed on the book while the instructor was reading, that organ, quicker than the ear and not easily controlled, would not always patiently accompany the reader word for word, but would outstrip the ear in apprehending the subject. Sometimes also a person less advanced, will be slow in following the teacher, or will stop to consider the words which are not familiar to him; so that, in either case, the learner would be unmindful of what is read, and the idea would be apprehended through the eye, not through the ear.

The learner also, occasionally perceiving letters which are not pronounced, would be apt to attribute his not hearing them to inattention or dulness of hearing on his part, and might still be inclined to introduce them in his pronunciation afterward. It is, therefore, better not to give the eye an opportunity of leading the ear astray. Besides, this dependence on the sight for understanding what is heard, incapacitates the ear for conversation, in which it can have no assistance from the eye.

By the reading of familiar subjects, suited to the age and proficiency of his pupils, the master will render them the same service as those who initiate us in childhood in the knowledge of our own language. But his mode of reading should be made a perfect fac-simile of that of speaking, by a natural and expressive delivery. Good reading is that which most nearly approaches extemporized speech. The interest with which a skilful instructor may invest this exercise by his manner of reading and the choice of subjects calculated to excite curiosity, will powerfully contribute to fix the attention of his hearers. He may always secure this point by calling on them, from time to time, to repeat or translate the last phrase he uttered.

The learners must now, while listening to the professor, mentally repeat after him. This direct association of the ideas with the sounds is the second step in the art of thinking in the language. The association of the spoken words with the ideas which they represent, offers no difficulty if the hearers have been accustomed to mental or direct reading; for it is impossible to follow a speaker and think with his words, unless the sounds awake the ideas. Direct hearing is therefore more necessary than direct reading: the latter operation is optional, the former is indispensable.

The fact that persons who, while able to read a foreign language, are yet unable to speak it, arises in a great measure from their not having contracted a habit of the association of words with ideas, by means of much practice in direct reading and hearing.

Perfection in audition, which consists in being able to understand oral discourse, however rapidly spoken, will be easily attained, if, by assiduous study, one has learned to read the foreign like the national authors, as quickly as the eye runs over the text; for the organs of speech utter the words more slowly than the eye peruses them. It must be borne in mind that the hearer has not, like the reader, the option of dwelling on an expression; he must apprehend the ideas of the speaker as they are delivered: he is completely at his mercy.

To reach this perfection, a *sine quâ non* in serious conversation, the pupils must desire the teacher to slacken or hurry his pace, as there is occasion. They should never hesitate to interrupt him, when they do not understand what he reads. The connection of the ideas will not suffer, as after every interruption the professor will resume his reading at the place where he stopped. The rarity of these interruptions will be a sure criterion of the progress of his pupils.

It would be otherwise if the instructor should prematurely address them in the foreign language; for their interruptions would be so many obstacles to his treating a subject connectedly. Thus, thwarted in his attempts, and frequently losing the thread of his discourse, he would soon be compelled to desist; whereas, with a book, he can always suit the simplicity of the subject and the slowness of his delivery, to the inexperience of his hearers. Moreover, reading renders improvement in the second branch independent of the oratorical powers of a teacher, who may be very deficient in this respect, at the same time that it familiarizes them with a better choice of words, a more correct phraseology, and a greater diversity of expression, than can be done in an extempore discourse. He could thus also store their minds with useful knowledge, and accustom them to all styles, to all modes of delivery, without himself possessing any other talent than that of reading.

A practice no less injudicious than that of prematurely addressing learners at some length in the foreign language, and one frequently resorted to, although at variance with the order of nature, is for the teacher to draw his pupils out into a conversation, when they are as yet unable to understand him. None but commonplace ideas could be ventured upon, and, owing to the difficulty of the attempt, considerable time would be lost; hence, very inadequate practice both in hearing and in speaking.

More objectionable still is conversation in a large class; for only a few of its members could seriously join in it, to the exclusion of the greater number, who, meanwhile, would remain completely idle. By reading, on the contrary, the professor can initiate in the comprehension of the spoken language fifty persons as easily as one. His discourse is addressed to all, and profits all. Those who have not had much practice will endeavor to catch the meaning of what they hear; the others will go further, and their attention will embrace both the pronunciation and the meaning. In any case, this exercise affords in a given time more practice in hearing than conversation.

Such is the merit of this process; it places the acquirement most essential for the exchange of ideas within reach of those whose limited resources will not allow them to obtain it except in large classes. It is well known that, when a great number of persons attend the same course of instruction, all cannot make the same progress: difference in age, aptitude, and taste, as well as in previous education, and the time they have at their disposal, will cause some to advance more rapidly than others. It is therefore important that the method should provide for this inequality among pupils of the same class.

As poetry does not admit of being translated extempore, the reading of it by the professor will, as it were, force the pupils to associate the thoughts directly with the words, and, at the same time, will be for them the best practical initiation into the prosody, if he carefully mark in reading the syllabic quantity and the tonic accent.

In this, as in every other department of the study of a language, practice should precede theory. It is only when the ear, by long experience, has been made conscious of the existence and nature of tones and quantity in syllables, that the mind can investigate melody and rhythm, that explanations can be given as to what constitutes the essence of verse, and the mechanism of the foreign versification.

The understanding of the spoken language in Italian, Spanish, and German, presents great facilities, owing to the correspondence between the pronunciation and the orthography. But the most difficult of all languages for a foreigner to understand is perhaps the English, on account of the complete absence of analogy in the alphabetical representation of its pronunciation, as well as of the rapidity with which it is spoken and its innumerable contractions.*

* This is humorously illustrated in the following anecdote: In a late trial before the Queen's Bench, Mr. Hawkins, a barrister, had frequently to advert to that description of vehicle called

Some people think that the French language is spoken faster than the English; this is a great error. Voltaire shrewdly observed, that an Englishman gains every day two hours on a Frenchman in conversation. The truth is, that English is spoken considerably quicker than French. This results from a difference of kind in the pronunciation of these languages.

Pronunciation is composed of two elements, vocal sounds and articulations, represented in writing by vowels and consonants. Vocal sounds admit of duration: quantity is their essence. Vocal articulations, with few exceptions, cannot be prolonged; instantaneity is their essence. When a consonant is placed after a vowel, it generally shortens it. Thus the long syllables,

brougham, which he pronounced in two syllables. Lord Campbell, the chief justice, suggested that the word was usually contracted to broom, and that he had better adopt the latter pronunciation, as he would thereby save one syllable and gain so much time. Henceforward Mr. Hawkins called it broom. Shortly after, the pleading turned upon omnibuses; and Lord Campbell frequently used the word omnibus, to which he gave its due length. "I beg your lordship's pardon," retorted Mr. Hawkins, "but, if you will call it bus, you will save two syllables, and make it more intelligible to the jury." The learned judge assented to the proposed abbreviation.

*me*, *we*, *fie*, *no*, *due*, *though*, become short by adding consonants to them, *met*, *web*, *fib*, *fit*, *fig*, *not*, *dun*, *thought*. Now, in English, consonants predominate, and usually form the end of syllables; hence a rapidity of utterance is the unavoidable consequence.

In French, on the contrary, consonants act but a secondary part, and are often silent. The spoken words, in reality, end with vowel-sounds, although consonants terminate their written representatives. In the division of the words, consonants seldom terminate syllables; the French word *caricature*, for example, is divided into syllables thus, că-rī-că-tū-rĕ; its pronunciation, conformably to this division, is necessarily longer than that of the English word, commonly pronounced, according to this other division, căr-ĭc-ă-tūre. The same may be said of every other word in the two languages. The vowels, which contribute so much to lengthen the words, are pronounced full in French, as if every syllable were accented. From these facts there necessarily results a slow and steady enunciation.

As the opinion of a foreigner, however, in regard to the English pronunciation, can have little weight, we beg to quote a few competent authorities: "Such is the vehemence of our accent, that every syllable which follows the accented is not only short, but almost lost in the pronunciation." (Lord Monboddo.) "We incline, in general, to a short pronunciation of our words, and have shortened the quantity of most of those which we borrowed from the Latin." (Hugh Blair.) "Such is the propensity for dispatch that, overlooking the majesty of words composed of many syllables aptly connected, the prevailing taste is to shorten words, so as to make them disagreeable to the ear." (Lord Kames.) "It must be regretted that contraction subjects our tongue to some of the most hissing, snapping, clashing sounds that ever grated the ear of a Vandal." (John Walker.) "Our rational conversation is, for the most part, carried on in a series of most extraordinary and rugged abbreviations, a species of short-hand talking." (Bulwer Lytton.)

But, whatever be the irregularities of the pronunciation or the rapidity of speech of a people, it is the business of learners to overcome the former, and accommodate themselves to the latter. Practice will suffice to enable the ear to distinguish the most delicate shades of sound; and the processes recommended above secure this object.

The professor who exercises his pupil in hearing has this great advantage over the mother who initiates her child in this department of the language, that the person he addresses, having a more mature understanding, must necessarily apprehend the ideas corresponding to the sounds more quickly and clearly than can be done by a young child through the language of action with which his mother accompanies her words. He owes his success to her admirable patience in repeating the same phrases, always associated with that language. The professor has, in translation and the previous reading of his pupils, no less powerful elements of success; and, if he exercises the same patience and the same perseverance in his teaching, he will obtain the same results in considerably less time.

Perseverance is equally indispensable, in order to preserve the acquisition. A language is, in fact, retained not in proportion to the degree of perfection attained, but to the length of time it has been practised, and to the strength of the habits contracted by the ear. The youngest children who are taken abroad lose their own language most rapidly, that is to say, according as they have heard the less of it.

When the language is perfectly understood, the professor will turn the proficiency of his pupils to account by always using it in speaking to them, even before they themselves speak it. The constant practice of following a train of ideas directly through the medium of words spoken by a native, will render the audible signs so familiar as soon to secure a habit of this mental operation; and, this once attained, it will cause these ideas, in virtue of the laws of association and habit, to be easily reproduced when the hearer has afterward need to convey them.

The pronunciation, thus directly associated with the thought, and daily becoming a firmer habit of the ear, the attention may be directed, while following the ideas, to the articulate sounds which represent them, as a preparation for the exercises in speaking, described in the following chapter. The faculty of reproducing the articulate sounds of a language, is the consequence of the frequent impressions made by them on the organ of hearing. Those are dumb to whom nature has refused the sense of hearing.

The accent, especially, which affects the whole tenor of discourse and consists in a vocal modulation peculiar to the nation, is fostered in the hearers by the reiterated impressions received from the foreign teacher's voice, if he reads as the language is usually spoken. The longer the ear is impressed with the national accent, the more its fibres vibrate in unison with it, and the greater is the power of the vocal organ to assimilate with it.

By the mode of proceeding which we have described above, a person possessing the art of reading a foreign language, would be able in six weeks, or two months at the most, to understand perfectly those who speak it, if he had at his command a reader, whether a professor or not, who should, for half an hour at a time, at short intervals, read to him the foreign language: and if he visited the country where it is spoken, he would have still greater facilities for understanding its inhabitants and adopting their pronunciation; a servant, a child even, who knows how to read, could rapidly forward him in this twofold acquirement. Success is, in any case, accessible to the most humble fortune; for the first art is learned without a master, and the second requires his services only for a very short time.

These two arts are so easily and speedily acquired, when, conformably to the laws of nature and of reason, their study is freed from all the fetters of routine, that one might in less than six months read and understand French, for instance, as well as a native. He could not, however, in as many years, learn to speak it like a Frenchman.

It is, therefore, most desirable that, among all civilized nations, the attention of youth should be more particularly directed to the first two arts, which, if universally diffused, would suffice, to the exclusion of the other two, for all the requirements of the international exchange of thought. Persons of different nations, each speaking or writing his own language, would understand each other, and their conversation would be the more expansive, the more satisfactory in every respect, as, in ordinary circumstances, ideas flow in the vernacular with more freedom and clearness than in a foreign idiom. In this way would the grand desideratum of modern society, international exchange of ideas, be secured.

The reciprocal knowledge of living languages cannot fail to extend our social relations and to render international intercourse more frequent and more useful; it would second the work of civilization, by promoting the progress of the arts and sciences, doing away with national prejudices, and drawing closer the bonds which ought to unite all the members of the great human family.

The literary and scientific celebrities, who popularize useful knowledge and new discoveries in public lectures, would be easily induced to visit neighboring countries, as they would then have every opportunity of collecting around them numerous hearers able to understand them. We do not, indeed, see why lecturers should not be patronized by an enlightened public, when foreign actors frequently perform to crowded auditories. Need we expatiate on the many advantages which, in a moral, intellectual, and social point of view, would accrue to society from this exchange of information and good offices.

Never was a common means of intellectual communication more needed than at the present day. Different communities, despite their rulers, tend to fraternize under the influence of similar institutions, similar pursuits, and similar tastes. The spirit of the age impels nations to form political and commercial alliances on all points of the globe, and to blend themselves into one great community. Scientific associations successively attract to the great centres of activity all the noblest intellects of the civilized world. Isolated labor is everywhere giving way to the spirit of association; and instead of wrapping their discoveries in secrecy, men of all countries diffuse them as means of universal advancement.

# CHAPTER IV.

## THE ART OF SPEAKING.

"Ici l'application serait meilleure que les règles, les exemples instruiraient mieux que les préceptes." BUFFON.

"Here practical application would be better than rules, examples more instructive than precepts."

As, in the present state of linguistic education, the first two arts, reading and hearing, are not universally diffused, the third, the art of speaking the foreign tongue, becomes invaluable for every person who comes in contact with foreigners unable to understand his language.

It is especially the case, after a foreign idiom has, like the native, become the direct instrument of the mind, that it promotes intellectual culture. The exchange of thought is, in fact, an essential element of improvement. In social intercourse, when a diversity of characters are brought together, every one contributes his share of knowledge, good sense, and experience, and all are gainers to some extent. If reading enriches the mind, conversation polishes and expands it. In conversing with those whose esteem we covet, or whom we would fain convert to our own way of thinking, the desire to please, to persuade, keeps all the faculties of the soul in a state of excitement, which multiplies the intellectual energies, and often leads to the conception of ideas, which would never have been evolved in the solitude of the study. It would, therefore, be wrong to neglect an art capable of producing such important results.

By reading and hearing, the student familiarizes himself with the models; by speaking and writing, he imitates them. The habit of receiving ideas directly from the words, written or spoken, lays the foundation for rapidly acquiring the faculty of expressing them spontaneously. The art of speaking thus finds infallible elements of success in the practice of the first two arts. But, without waiting until perfection is gained in these, the learners will pass on to the exercises of the third. With this view, they must imitate the pronunciation of their professor, and the phraseology of standard authors.

The task of the instructor, as regards pronunciation, should consist less in correcting his pupils' errors than in preventing them from committing any. Prevention is better than cure. As a general rule, they ought never to pronounce a word, unless they have heard it several times. So long as the organs do not practise any pronunciation, they remain ready to acquire a good one; but a bad habit once contracted, is eradicated with difficulty.

There will be no danger of falling into a defective pronunciation, if, following the law of nature, as manifested in infancy, the pupil listens to his master a long time before attempting to imitate him. The exercises of the preceding chapter, having formed the ear to correct habits, the vocal organs will be in a favorable state for giving the true pronunciation. The vocal faculty is governed by the ear; there are no articulate sounds perceptible to the organ of hearing which the voice cannot reproduce.

Pronunciation is most commonly taught by imposing on a beginner the oral reading of the foreign text, that is, making him infer it from the orthography—a mode of proceeding doubly irrational, as it rejects imitation in an art exclusively based on this power, and as it implies that the thing signified, not previously known, can be learned from its sign. It moreover submits the pronunciation to the learner's attention without regard to the meaning of the words, although their pronunciation often varies with their signification. For instance, the pronunciation of the words *bow*, *gill*, *read*, *desert*, *gallant*, *conjure*, *rebel*, *minute*, and many others, depends on the sense in which they are taken. It is the same in other languages, though the English, especially, abounds in words which differ in pronunciation, according to their meaning.

Reason dictates that the means should be consistent with the end; but reading aloud is precisely the reverse of what takes place in conversation. In speaking, we pass from the idea to the word; the sound suggests the orthography: in reading, on the contrary, we pass from the word to the idea; the orthography suggests the sound. Reading aloud can only be a source of errors for a beginner. The correction to which it leads could not create good habits: these result alone from reiterated correct impressions, such as arise from the processes explained in the foregoing chapter. Its proper office is to test the progress made in pronunciation.

The two readings by the master, as explained in the preceding chapter, were intended to initiate the learners in the understanding of the spoken language, and to accustom the ear to a good pronunciation. He will now make them enter on the practice of the latter by reading the same passages twice more—the first time very slowly, and by short phrases of three or four words, which they will repeat after him without looking at the text, and in imitation not only of the sounds, prosodial accent, and blending of the words, but also of the intonation and inflection of voice peculiar to the people.

These imitations should, as in acquiring the native tongue, be made without reference to the alphabetical characters. Whenever the pupils fail in reproducing the exact pronunciation or accentuation of their model, it is a proof they need to hear it again. The professor will, therefore, at each failure, utter the words anew. The voice, that docile slave of the ear, in order to echo the pronunciation faithfully, only needs to have it clearly impressed on this organ.

In his second reading, which will be uninterrupted, he will set the example of a correct delivery by an accentuation conformable to the habits of speaking of well-informed people. His hearers, previously familiarized with the spoken language, having now heard the same passage read four times in succession, will experience no difficulty in associating mentally the pronunciation with the ideas.

When, by means of these imitations, a student has a complete mastery of all the elementary sounds of the foreign language, he will direct his attention to the alphabetical signs which represent them, and will find it both easy and interesting to attach to the written words, as is done in the maternal idiom, a pronunciation perfectly familiar to him. He may then occasionally read the same passage which the professor has now read four times, and, in doing so, will direct his attention exclusively to the ideas, in order to deliver the text naturally and with the inflections of voice required on the subject. The pronunciation is not known until it has become so fixed a habit, that, in speaking or reading, it is produced spontaneously and without diverting the mind from the thought.

We will here observe that these four readings are, in their nature and effect, precisely identical with what takes place, as already seen, in the first four periods of our apprenticeship to the vernacular idiom. The child first seizes on the ideas with the aid of the language of action, which accompanies the short phrases addressed to him; he is soon able without this assistance to understand continuous speech on matters within the scope of his intelligence; next, he tries to pronounce the words and phrases he has most frequently heard; and, at last, when, by speaking, the pronunciation has grown familiar to him, he is taught to read.

Of the four readings given by the professor, the first and third, in detached phrases, being intended only to initiate the pupils, the first, in comprehending, the third, in pronouncing the language, need not be continued for any length of time. But consecutive reading will be persevered in, in order to confirm the learners in good habits of pronunciation: according to their progress, this reading will become more rapid and be continued longer at a time.

When, both from hearing and from reading, accurate impressions have, by repetition, grown familiar to the mind, any deviation from them, which one may afterward meet, would strike him as being incorrect. This consciousness of propriety, arising from the habit of the ear or the eye, as formed in good society or from good books, is a practical conviction, a true experimental knowledge, and our best guide in the expression of thought. Good speakers and good writers are guided by the ear rather than by rules.

It may sometimes be desirable to commence the exercises of pronunciation at an early period of the study. There is nothing to prevent it, although it is never advisable to act contrary to the dictates of nature; but, at whatever period they are entered upon, it is indispensable to pronounce only words which are fully understood, and have been frequently heard.

In a language the orthography of which faithfully represents the pronunciation, the written and the articulate words, being easily inferred one from the other, will not only render reading and hearing mutual auxiliaries, but will enable the student to arrive, by analogy, at the pronunciation of the whole language from that of a few words.

Reading aloud, unavailable in most languages, as a means of learning pronunciation, will serve to keep it up at a later period, when once perfectly acquired. A good habit of pronunciation may likewise be kept up by storing the memory with select passages of prose and poetry. The possibility of repeating them at any time and in any place offers an easy means of obtaining that correct and natural enunciation which is the crowning perfection in the pronunciation of a language.

When reiterated imitation shall have enabled the learners to reproduce faithfully and naturally the pronunciation of their model, that is, when it shall have become habitual to them—the professor will lead them to another kind of imitation, that of the foreign phraseology—an exercise the easier as the attention is free from any consideration of pronunciation.

The arts of speaking and writing are acquired by the same process as that which leads to excellence in other arts. Imitation and practice can alone in all arts produce a good execution. It is as irrational to make grammar the starting-point in learning to speak, as it would be to, impose on a child the study of perspective or the theory of colors as the preliminary step to learning the art of painting. In both, practice, founded on example, is the basis of improvement. Practice alone may, by induction, lead to a knowledge of grammar; the latter can never of itself lead to practice.

If, as already shown, the knowledge of the second class of words is a useful auxiliary in learning to understand the foreign text, it must be equally useful when we wish to express our thoughts. Those are, in fact, the words which enable us to vary the phraseology indefinitely. The professor ought, therefore, to have them before him, when exercising his pupils, that he may readily introduce them into the sentences which he gives them in their own language for construction in the foreign one. The learners, on their part, when thoroughly masters of the pronunciation, will find no difficulty in committing them to memory, as they become familiar by frequent recurrence in reading and hearing.

A previous knowledge of the verbs is equally useful in the first steps toward the art of speaking. This word *par excellence*, constituted, as it is in cultivated languages, with its moods, tenses, persons, numbers, and inflections, is the most ingenious of instituted signs, the vital element of discourse, and the masterpiece of language. It expresses in itself a judgment and a proposition. Its inflections are, in some languages, so numerous that a very long time would be required to know them all by practice only. It is, therefore, useful to make them an object of study, chiefly with a view to learning the different relations which they express. Let it be remembered that an acquaintance with words or the import of their inflections does not imply the study of grammar, which more properly consists in definitions, rules, and disquisitions on language.

The verb is truly the essence of the proposition: without it we can neither affirm, deny, nor question; it will necessarily form part of every sentence, which the master gives his pupils as models, to exercise them in the phraseological variations. We can speak from the moment we know one verb perfectly, and can unhesitatingly apply it in every possible manner without reference to the mother-tongue.

If it be considered that a verb in all its moods, tenses, and persons, and in its various forms, active, passive, and reflective, affirmative, interrogative, and negative, presents above a *thousand* distinct propositions, it will clearly appear that, by successively joining to it the other elements of speech, an inexhaustible diversity of expressions may be produced. By changing the words of the second class, we obtain different modifications of the same idea; and, by varying those of the first, we express different ideas under similar circumstances.

The thought undergoes at pleasure an endless metamorphosis, and the vocal organs acquire corresponding flexibility. Each new verb introduces a new series of ideas, and opens a boundless field for practice. Diversity in unity is one of the great laws of nature.

Isolated verbs present but vague ideas; they require to be incorporated in phrases which determine their meaning. The learners, after conjugating a verb with the master, so as to make sure of its pronunciation, if not already completely known, must, at first, with his aid, then alone, join words to it in all its moods and tenses, attaching thereto, directly and mentally, the ideas conveyed by these combinations. The conjugation of propositions, both useful and interesting, supplies memory with the materials of conversation; whereas the monotonous task of conjugating the verb by itself presents no distinct idea to the mind, and affords no help toward speaking. Hence it is, that the ablest teachers at the present day exercise their pupils on the verbs in the way we suggest.

Learners, beside forming different phrases on the same verb, should compose variations on the model phrases, which the professor selects from what he has read to them. This exercise is superior to the first; because it leads them from the known to the unknown, and presents to them, not words with which to form phrases, but sentences to be decomposed into their elements and recomposed by imitation. The professor will give the preference to those expressions which elucidate points of grammar, especially those which differ in their construction in the two languages, taking care in these variations to preserve the syntactic or idiomatic character of the model-phrase.

If his pupils hesitate, they should be at once assisted either by his recalling to their memory the model-phrase, or stating the grammatical rule which governs it, as also by constructing for them a part or the whole of the sentences proposed. When seasonable assistance is afforded to them, more sentences are formed in a given time, the syntactical construction of the language becomes very familiar, and the words are learned with their proper pronunciation, by being repeatedly heard from the instructor.

This exercise is the counterpart of that for

teaching how to understand the spoken language as described in the last chapter. The master then formed phraseological combinations in his own language; he now forms them in the language of the learners, for them to translate into his. But, in the present exercise, the introduction of a great number of new words is not so favorable to progress as the reiterated use of those already known. What is required for the exchange of thought is not so much the names of things as the power of affirming, denying, and questioning respecting them; one must especially be able to adapt the foreign phraseology to the requirements of thought, and reproduce it in conversation with the spontaneousness of the native idiom. The vocabulary of young children is very limited; and, yet, how readily and fluently they speak!

To exercise the judgment and invention, and to afford learners opportunities of applying whatever knowledge they acquire, should be the constant endeavor of an instructor. Half the knowledge with twice the power of applying it, is better than twice the knowledge with only half the power of application.

The model-phrases must, at first, be very simple, but always complete and composed of elements familiar to the learners, in order that they may turn their attention exclusively to the construction. The master will modify them, by substituting for the words which enter into their composition other words of the same species, changing the moods, tenses, and persons of the verbs, putting an interrogative or negative proposition for an affirmative, and *vice versa;* adding adverbs, conjunctions, and other words as they advance. He can always proportion the difficulty to his pupils' proficiency, and give them the explanations they want; but each new word he introduces must be dwelt upon in order to render its application familiar and fix it in their memory. This practical syntax is thus doubly beneficial; but what makes it still more so in public instruction is, that the sentences proposed to each learner, not having been committed to memory, are so many problems, the solution of which interests the whole class.

Every question should be asked before naming the learner who will have to answer it. By this means all the members of a class, in the expectation of being called upon, will be induced to listen attentively, and, under the stimulus of emulation, will call forth their mental powers. Each will thus contribute, by the force of example, to the progress of the others, which is not the case when they repeat a lesson learned by all.

In order, with still more effect, to direct the attention of his pupils to what characterizes the genius of the foreign language, in the model-phrases offered for their imitation, the professor will write each of them, or have them written on the blackboard; then, after making sure that all the members of the class understand it perfectly, he will exercise them in making similar ones, as already explained, adducing rules in aid of the practice, whenever required.

As a prelude to this exercise, the professor will, at first, confine his pupils to the bare imitation of the text he reads to them. After each phrase which he gives them to translate, as explained in the preceding chapter, he will call on them to reproduce the original from their own version, phrase by phrase. Having the text before him, he could easily correct their errors, even if he was not thoroughly master of the language he teaches. This second translation, as it requires a knowledge of the pronunciation, more particularly suits the Latin, in which it may be had recourse to at every stage of the learner's progress.

But the reproduction of a text in a language which is to be spoken, is not sufficient for the requirements of conversation. We should have it in our power to vary the form of every sentence. It is by analogy that model-phrases can be modified so as to reproduce similar ones, and thus to multiply indefinitely the expression of thought. The learner will then practise making variations on the text, and will modify every sentence in a hundred ways before he parts with it. The repetition of the same forms, thus applied to ever-varying ideas, is both impressive and recreative.

It is in living languages especially that the exercise in phraseology presents great facilities; for the teacher can always supply from his own resources abundant materials. If he is a man of education and a native of the country, the language of which he teaches, he can generally determine, without reference to books, the forms of expression which are admissible, and the precise ideas which, in different cases, are attached to words.

The model-phrase being previously known, the exercise here recommended conforms to these vital principles—*the idea before the sign, and the phrase before the words;* it possesses also this great advantage: while the judgment is directed to the idiomatic arrangement of the words, the memory lays hold of them as a necessary consequence of their frequent recurrence in the various modifications which the same sentence undergoes, and lays hold of them in an order conformable to the genius of the language.

Jacotot, the originator of "Universal Teaching," and other eminent professors after him, exercise their pupils on these variations; but, for the most part, they confine themselves to one text, and to a very limited number of ideas and expressions. Nevertheless, they are on the right road; we only suggest a more extensive application of their method, a phraseology more diversified.

Analogy, which presides over the formation of phrases, is an imitation modified by judgment: it produces similar forms; whereas, imitation reproduces the forms themselves. It is a logical process with its premises and its consequences, a species of rule of three in which the fourth term of a proportion is to be discovered. If, for instance, the French of *I am hungry* is *j'ai faim*, what is the French of *he is hungry*, *you are hungry, are you hungry*, etc.? The solution of these questions is a logical consequence for any one who knows the French verb *être* (to be).

With a thorough knowledge of the conjugations and the pronunciation, these oral compositions may be entered upon at any period of the study. If regularly practised at short intervals, they will gradually be delivered with greater decision and fluency; and a close association will soon be established between the thought and the phrase, which fixes the latter in the mind and begets the faculty of reproducing it spontaneously, of thinking aloud, as it were, in the foreign language.

Translation, in oral expression, is attended with the same inconvenience which is attached to it in the first two arts, from the want of identically corresponding terms in the two languages. In colloquial intercourse no time is allowed for the operation; its tediousness could not but be painful to impatient hearers. Unless the exchange of ideas is direct, there can be no genuine conversation. Direct speaking will be the more effectually accomplished, if the learner, conforming to the order prescribed by reason in the successive acquisition of the different departments of a foreign language, has previously associated ideas with the words by direct reading and direct hearing.

There is no reading-book which does not present abundant forms of speech fit to serve as models, and which could not familiarize a learner with most of the peculiarities of the language. leading him, by analogous constructions, from the simplest phrase to the most complicated proposition, giving him, in short, the power of modifying the expression according to the requirements of thought, an advantage never to be gained from the dialogues which young people are often compelled to commit to memory. A person learns to speak, to extemporize, not by reciting ready-made phrases, but by forming them himself by analogy, and adapting them to the ideas he has to express. The acquisitions of memory are limited; those of judgment are without bounds.

Numerous collections of dialogues and detached phrases have been compiled for the use of learners; but why should their power of expression be restricted to such fragments of conversation? What need is there for all these books of phrases, when good writers abound in expressions perfectly correct, while their application is rendered striking and easy by the very text of which they are a part? Besides, the automatic association of words, learned in a given order, creates a habit which forbids their being availed of in the diversified circumstances of social intercourse.

A judicious selection of phrases may, however, become a powerful auxiliary for the manifestation of thought, if, instead of learning it by heart and adhering exclusively to the text, the learner be exercised in expressing his own ideas by numerous modifications of its phraseology, which render the foreign idiom familiar to the mind.

By learning a phrase, the student exercises his memory; but, by constructing one himself, he exercises his judgment. In the first case he only knows that phrase; in the second he learns with the phrase the rule by which it is formed. By the first exercise he repeats a lesson; by the second he speaks. In learning dialogues one tries to retain foreign phrases corresponding to the native, without having occasion to inquire into the genius of either language, while the practice of phrase-making obliges the learner to compare the constructions of the corresponding sentences.

The decomposition of model-phrases, in order to reconstruct others of the same kind, is a felicitous application of the analytical method, which leads from the whole to its parts, and by which we become thoroughly acquainted with the functions of the words, the import of their inflections, and the relations existing between them—considerations no less important for accuracy of thought than for propriety of expression.

A good collection of dialogues would, however, present this practical advantage, that, abounding in phrases of daily use, no time would be lost in search of those which are most wanted in ordinary intercourse. It would forward the learner's progress in familiar conversation, provided he should modify them variously in direct association with the ideas. With a perfect knowledge of pronunciation and analogy for a guide, an adult especially can practise by himself phraseological variations which embody ideas directly. This exercise does not come within the province of a teacher, who can assist his pupils in the construction of foreign sentences only by a reference to the corresponding expressions in their native tongue. In fact, the only departments of a language for which an earnest learner, with a due share of common sense, really requires the aid of a teacher, are audition and pronunciation; for every thing else he can dispense with and think for himself.

Analogy enables us to adapt the form of expression to the requirements of the thought; it is the light of language, its vital principle; it presides over its formation, and greatly facilitates its intelligibility, use, and acquisition. When custom is doubtful, analogy decides. To establish analogies is the first exercise of the judgment: it is the kind of reasoning most accessible to all capacities. Throughout life we form new phrases from those we have heard or read. Analogy is the very soul of the phraseological exercises we recommend; those who will resort to them with perseverance will acquire the habit of speaking in conformity with the genius of the language. The numerous applications we make of this power in acquiring our own render its action so instantaneous that it passes unperceived; this accounts for its being so generally neglected in the teaching of languages.

The learning of grammar, with a view to conform to the genius of a language, is contrary to the dictates of nature and reason; since, as was shown, it places precept before example, theory before practice. The learner must study the facts themselves, not the rules which have been deduced from them. A foreign language ought undoubtedly to be known grammatically; but this does not mean that it should be learned through grammar; it means that it should be spoken and written conformably to the practice of the best speakers and writers. If we reflect that grammarians do not impose laws, but only state, within certain limits, what is the common usage among those who speak and write well, it will be obvious that the readiest and most direct way of ascertaining this usage is to frequent the society of well-educated people and study the best writers. We shall thus learn from them, as the grammarians themselves have done, what constitutes correct expression. Custom is the arbiter of language, and, consequently, should be our guide in its acquisition. In speaking or writing a foreign idiom, we ought to be able, as in the vernacular, to ascertain the right pronunciation, orthography, gender, inflection, grammatical concord, and order of words, by an appeal to our consciousness of their correctness, resulting from reiterated impressions, rather than to our recollection of rules.

The rapidity of speech in extempore speaking does not permit rules of any kind to be applied:

the words should flow in their right order, not by the aid of reasoning, but instantaneously, from a sentiment of analogy, and as the immediate consequence of the thought. There is no time for thinking about the details of composition or pronunciation in the very act of speaking; the mind being then preoccupied with the ideas, their connection, and subordination. An art is fully known only when practised without reference to its elements or principles.

Those, however, who aim at a systematic knowledge of the foreign grammar must, when sufficiently advanced, study its rules and put them in practice by numerous applications, taking as models the examples which accompany them. It is not by learning, but by applying the rules, that grammar is really known. This is an exercise of the judgment vastly more interesting and beneficial, in every respect, than mnemonic lessons of grammar. The multiplicity of these applications, by rendering the syntactic forms habitual, will fix the laws of the language indelibly in the mind. Nothing is well known until it is well understood; and the best way to understand a thing is to put it in practice.

If, for example, a great diversity of sentences

be formed with French verbs requiring either *à* or *de* after them, the perplexity which these prepositions present will soon disappear by that practice; and learners will use them, as it were, instinctively by the force of habit and analogy. In the same way, also, a practical acquaintance with the genders of nouns would be easily gained in the same language which attributes to the names of inanimate objects a masculine or feminine, devoid of any distinctive marks by which it can be known, and whose articles and adjectives vary in their terminations to indicate their concord with the substantives preceded by articles and other determinatives, or joined to various adjectives, associations would be formed in the mind of the student, which would enable him to use the proper gender spontaneously and unconsciously, as do the French themselves. In this manner all the grammatical forms of a language would soon be rendered familiar.

The same may be said of idiomatic phrases: let a student, for instance, apply the French expression, *perdre quelqu'un de vue* (to lose sight of any one), to a sufficient number of phrases to render the construction habitual, he will not be liable to forget it, and afterward fall into the bar-

barism of a literal translation of the corresponding English phrase. The power of expression will arise from the frequency and diversity of these applications.

Repetition is necessary to produce lasting impressions on the brain; hence the power of speaking arises from habits engendered by patient practice; and, as the professor cannot always, in his lessons, devote to the phraseological exercise the time required for imparting to his pupils the facility and variety of expression which thoughts demand, he will give them, or they will themselves select from a book, the model-phrases on which, in the intervals of the lessons, they will write and make *viva voce* analogous variations.

The phraseological constructions which the student practises by himself, are the fittest to secure to him the power of speaking the foreign language. But, to this effect, he must, when exercising himself in the absence of the professor, carefully avoid forming the sentences in his own language for translation into the other. He will express the ideas directly in the latter, that is, will think aloud in it. After a few successful attempts in this, the transition to carrying on mentally a train of thoughts will present no difficulty, especially to one who can follow directly the ideas of a book or of a speaker.

There can be no conversation on a connected subject, unless the thought be embodied directly in the language. The working of the mind in the act of translating impedes the exchange of ideas in speaking as well as in listening; it checks the movements of the heart, under whose inspirations are manifested the intonation of the voice and the expression of the countenance, so indispensable to the force and clearness of oral discourse.

In order the more certainly to make the foreign language the vehicle of his ideas, the student, speaking to himself as a child does when talking to her doll, will connect together familiar phrases—affirming and denying, questioning and answering in turns—carrying on, in fact, various trains of ideas as prompted by his imagination. He will, in these monologues, introduce the words and phrases he knows best, and which flow naturally from his lips with tones and inflections of voice that harmonize with what passes in his mind.

The written exercise, which will serve at the same time as a preparation for the art of writing, should precede the oral exercise, if the organs of hearing and speech have not yet been sufficiently exercised in pronunciation. In any case the two exercises will assist each other.

If a person, having once acquired a language, perseveres in these exercises, conjointly with direct reading, he will preserve—nay, more, will indefinitely extend his knowledge of it. Habit, not skill in the practice of an art. is the means of never forgetting it.

Although, in our ordinary social relations, the exchange of thought is chiefly effected by detached phrases, we sometimes have occasion to unfold at some length our ideas, to relate facts and incidents. Passing, therefore, from detached phrases to connected discourse, and from translation to the direct expression of thought, the learners will acquire the talent of speaking extempore in the foreign language, as they would in their own, by relating anecdotes, historical facts, remarkable events, or other narratives, very short at first, and becoming gradually longer as their proficiency increases. He who has, one day, spoken for ten minutes, has surmounted a difficulty, and will be able, another day, to speak for fifteen minutes. So will this invaluable talent progress.

The student will take the subject-matter of his narrations from works written in the language he is learning; but he must be careful not to make them mere lessons of memory. To recite is one thing, to speak another. The learner should never parrot words in a given order, but should deliver his narrative as an original language of his own, a task which presents no difficulty at this advanced stage. In studying his subject he must, therefore, pay more attention to his ideas than to the manner in which they are conveyed, to the succession of incidents rather than of the words, and afterward relate the story in his own way, availing himself of the author's phraseology only when it comes without effort as the direct expression of his ideas, and even modifying the incidents or substituting others when memory fails.

In a class all the learners may prepare the same narrative, and each, in turn, deliver some portion of it. Should they be sufficiently advanced to enter upon this exercise, and yet feel diffident, they ought to select subjects which are familiar to their instructor, thereby enabling him to aid their recollection. The professor, by skilfully catechising them respecting the characters and incidents of the story, through the medium of the foreign language itself, would elicit from them the whole matter. In an advanced class, considerable interest and benefit would accrue from the introduction by the more forward learners of narratives not previously known to their class-fellows.

Narration is in a foreign, as in the native idiom, the best preparation for extemporaneous speaking, and no less useful as a means of intellectual culture than necessary in social intercourse. It yields in importance to no other exercise. It appeals to the judgment as well as to the memory, by directing attention to the language of the author, and also to the connected facts of the narrative, to portraits of characters and descriptions of places. It fosters in a class self-confidence and presence of mind, without which words and ideas are unavailing for public speaking. It possesses also this advantage, as an exercise in pronunciation, that the latter is naturally associated with the ideas, whereas, in oral reading, it is irrationally made a consequence of the orthography.

The professor will again promote the progress of his pupils in extempore speaking, if he reads or delivers to them narratives, descriptions, or any interesting discourses which, while exhibiting to them the proper way of treating a subject, will also set them the example of correct diction and good pronunciation. Success depends on the frequency of the efforts made to reproduce what has been read or heard.

It is a common saying that, to learn to speak, one should speak much: this is not sufficient; imitation of what is read and heard is far more conducive to improvement in that art than the act itself of speaking. Mere practice in the latter imparts volubility in dealing out one's stock of materials; it does not enrich the mind with one word, one idea.

It has been shown that reading to learners is preferable to conversing with them, as a means of initiating them into the art of hearing; so is narrating preferable to joining in conversation as a means of learning to speak. It affords greater facilities for the intelligent imitation of good models and the delivery of long discourses; whereas, the use of monosyllables and detached phrases being optional in conversation, the learner might not make the efforts necessary for long periods. The instructor, owing to his greater power of expression, would probably engross the conversation to himself, so that the desired end would not be attained. Even, if the pupil took an equal share in it, he would also speak less in a given time than in narration.

The latter presents this other advantage, that the professor, having neither to supply the subject of conversation, nor to answer his pupil, would give his attention exclusively to the manner of his delivery, and might thus correct all his errors. The case would be quite different in conversation. To keep it from flagging, the professor would neglect the manner for the matter; his mind being preoccupied with what he should say, or what replies he should give, the pupil's mistakes would pass unnoticed, and might become a habit.

No conversation is possible, unless one can speak with sufficient ease and correctness not to give occasion for frequent interruptions, caused by hesitation in the choice of words and forms of speech, or by the correction of errors in pronunciation or construction. These interruptions diverting attention from the subject to the words, would be equally discouraging for the pupil and fatiguing for the master: they would render serious conversation almost impossible.

Besides, what conversation can there be between a master and his pupils? The very little that the latter could say would never afford sufficient practice to gain an extensive range of colloquial language. They meet, the one to communicate; the others, to receive instruction; the former ought to speak; the latter, to listen.

As to those unconnected, commonplace conversations which daily arise from the familiar intercourse of life, and for which dialogues are a sort of preparation, they do not require any extensive knowledge of a language, nor any remarkable conversational powers. An intelligible pronunciation and the most ordinary phraseology are amply sufficient. It is worthy of remark that, in in this familiar exchange of ideas, the ignorant speak more than the learned, and fools more than men of sense. The loquacity of young children and servant-maids is proverbial. Descartes must have alluded to this kind of talk when he said, "Mere speaking does not require much judgment."

As an introduction to this colloquial talk, learners may be asked in the foreign language itself various questions illustrative of the verb or the model-phrase, which is in course of practice;

and, by substituting the affirmative or negative proposition for the interrogative used by the professor, they will find no difficulty in giving the answers in the very words and idiomatical or syntactical construction of the questions.

With a higher aim in view and at a more advanced period, if the professor has sufficient leisure to converse more at length with his pupils, and has not present to his mind a fit subject in which the latter can join, we will suggest that every object within reach or within sight may supply matter for instructive conversation. An enlightened teacher can always draw out his pupils by questioning them on the forms, colors, dimensions, and other properties of any article whatever, on its value, origin, mode of fabrication, and on the substances which enter into its composition. By the relations which this article may bear to others, he will be led to conversing with them on a great number of things, which cannot fail to extend their vocabulary and enlarge the sphere of their ideas.*

Let the professor be received as a friend in the

See "Language as a Means of Mental Culture and International Communication." Book IV., Chapter II. Conversations on Objects.

family of his pupils; they will then have the opportunity to put into practice in his society the knowledge which he has imparted to them of his language. In any case, connected conversations can be practised only in social intercourse and in private teaching; they are next to impossible in large classes. The members of those must resort to narrations, to which they may add recapitulations of their readings. These exercises so very superior to conversation, as means of unfolding the talent of speaking, will, at the same time that they afford an opportunity of turning to advantage the acquirements gained by the practice of the first two arts, exercise their fellow-students in the understanding of the spoken language.

At this last stage of their studies, they can commit but few mistakes in speaking, and should not, therefore, be deterred by any motive from joining in conversation. Self-confidence is the basis of success in every art. From the moment they use the foreign language with any degree of expertness, their further improvement will be carried on, as in their own, by frequent intercourse with the well-educated, the reading of the great writers, and due attention to precepts on the oratorical art. But it is not to be expected that, in ordinary circumstances, a person will be able to acquire at home a complete knowledge of all the idioms and delicacies of a foreign language, or command of expression adequate to the elaborate discussion of serious subjects. Great powers of elocution are rare in the native and rarer still in a foreign idiom.

The different exercises we have sketched, by which learners are led from their first initiation in the understanding of the spoken language, in pronunciation, phrase-making, and narration, to the complete possession of these different departments, demand the active coöperation of master and pupil. They must alternate at intervals, proportioned in length to the age of the learners. The prolonged action of the faculties on one and the same subject fatigues them and produces inattention. A change of occupation is indispensable to renew their energy.

Students will be less subject to fatigue and listlessness, as we have suggested, if they are of an age to take pleasure in the work allotted to them, and, especially, if they have gained the talent of direct reading. It is in this case only that the professor can really take an active part in their studies, and that they will derive from his services all the advantages to be expected therefrom.

The great talent of the master lies in exciting his pupils to study, in leading them to voluntary efforts, and in making them feel the necessity of the tasks imposed on them. When he has once put them in the right track, their progress will thenceforth depend only on their perseverance in following the prescriptions of nature. The greatest service a professor can render his pupils is to make them independent of him.

Some persons lament that they have not a talent for learning languages: this is often but a plea for a want of energy, of perseverance, but also because they know not how to proceed in the study. Man has been created a communicative being, and has been endowed with the means of accomplishing his destiny. Every language is accessible to his intellect, and its pronunciation to his organs; all that he requires is the will and a good method: a child with a lever is stronger than Hercules abandoned to his own strength.

## CHAPTER V.

### THE ART OF WRITING.

"Iter est longum per præcepta, breve et efficax per exempla."

SENECA.

IN the ordinary circumstances of life we have less frequent occasion to write than to speak. The necessity for composition in a foreign language is almost entirely confined to epistolary purposes; and very few are those who, being acquainted with a foreign language, have correspondents abroad. With the exception of diplomatists and merchants, out of a hundred persons who learn foreign languages, not two perhaps ever have need of writing them. Besides, the fear of not expressing one's thoughts clearly, or of making blunders, often deters persons from turning this talent to account.

Nevertheless, the art of writing, though of limited utility as an ultimate object, is a powerful auxiliary to the acquiring of a critical and complete knowledge of a language. The exercises necessary for improvement in the art of writing a foreign language, will enable a student, without a master's aid, to become well acquainted with the spelling, concord, and arrangement of words, and to apply the rules of the language to the expression of thought, as he learns them. This art is the more easily acquired, as, like that of reading, it can be practised in the master's absence, being based exclusively on the imitation of good writers.

The various exercises recommended for learning the art of speaking, are also applicable to that of writing. The student who understands the foreign tongue, both written and spoken, without translating, ought always, when attempting the construction of phrases, either orally or in writing, to attach to them their correlative ideas, without the intervention of the corresponding expressions of his own idiom. In proceeding thus gradually from the simplest to the most complicated propositions, from detached sentences to connected discourse, he will soon be able to compose directly, that is, to think in writing that language.

The greater the proficiency attained in the arts of reading, hearing, and speaking, the greater the success in the exercises which have composition for their object. This is the order dictated by reason, but reversed by routine despite common sense. To attempt writing a language without previous extensive reading, is wishing to reap without having sown, to know without having learned. The exercises compiled for the avowed object of applying rules at the outset of the study, are purely mechanical, and can end only in disgust and failure. We should tax any one with insanity, who should insist on teaching a child to write his own language before he had learned to read; is it not far more unreasonable and absurd to compel a learner to write in a language of which he has not yet the least practical knowledge?

Imitation being the basis of progress in this art, recourse must not be had, in the first instance, to grammar, which only gives precepts, but to a good author who may be used as a model. His text, while exhibiting the rule embodied in the example, presents the words with their orthography and their true meanings; it teaches, in addition to syntax, all that constitutes the merit of style. It also dispenses, and this is not one of its least advantages, with the use of the dictionary, which is still more perplexing in writing a foreign language, than in translating into one's own.

It was by studying the works of their predecessors that the most distinguished authors learned to write. Many of them have declared the fact in their works, and, eager to benefit us by their experience, have earnestly recommended the practice of reading. "Plato," says Longinus, who himself holds the same opinion, "has taught us that the surest means of attaining perfection in style, is to imitate and emulate eminent writers." D'Alembert exclaims, "What precepts are preferable to the study of great models?"—"The assiduous reading of good writings," says Voltaire, "will be more useful for the formation of a pure and correct style, than the study of our grammars. We soon acquire the habit of speaking well by the frequent reading of those who have written well." One of our most eloquent writers, J. J. Rousseau, also says: "I give you no other rules for writing well, than the books which are well written. . . . . It is a law of nature that our minds insensibly imbibe a coloring from those with whom we associate, whether they are brought in contact by the living voice or the written page." Demosthenes, in order to improve his style, transcribed eight times the "Peloponnesian War" of Thucydides. When Lord Clarendon was engaged in writing his history, he was constantly studying Livy and Tacitus. The latter classic was also the favorite author of Montesquieu. Again, Benjamin Franklin, adopting Dr. Johnson's opinion, made the *Spectator* of Addison his model-book. Byron acknowledged what he owed to Pope, when he mentioned him, in one of his letters, as "the delight of his boyhood and the study of his manhood." Boileau declares himself the imitator of Horace. Dante took Virgil for his model: "Thou art my master and my author," he exclaims in his sublime poem; "it is from thee alone I took that beautiful style which has done me honor."

The best mode of imitation in foreign composition is *double-translation,* which consists in translating the foreign text into the national idiom, and then endeavoring to reproduce that text by translating the version back into the original.

The *vivâ voce* double-translation, recommended in the preceding chapter, was made phrase by phrase, and consequently only taught how to express detached ideas; the present exercise, having for its object the formation of style, is performed on passages increasing in length with the learner's progress, and will lead to the writing of connected discourse.

This imitative process can be easily adapted to all degrees of proficiency. Besides exercising the learner in the composition of his own, as well as of the foreign language, it supplies the means of correcting mistakes in the latter, by comparing his second translation with the author's text, which, if judiciously chosen, is the safest guide that can be followed.

Double-translation is not an innovation; it is recommended by Cicero, Pliny the Younger, Quintilian, and nearly all those who, to the present day, have suggested means for acquiring the arts of writing and speaking in a second language. It is chiefly by means of this exercise that Queen Elizabeth, as Roger Ascham, her tutor, tells us, learned the Latin language, which she spoke so freely. The historian Gibbon declares that he gained, through double-translation, an extensive knowledge of Latin and French, and the command of a correct style in English.

Its principle is generally recognized in classical instruction; the Latin exercises given to boys, are usually imitations of the classical texts, which they have already construed. Its utility is not restricted to the idioms of ancient times, and of modern Europe; Sir William Jones asserts that, "by double-translation more Arabic and Persian will be learned in ten months, than can be learned in ten years by any other method."

The difficulty of the task must always be proportioned to the proficiency of the pupils; no exercise ought to be either so difficult as to discourage their efforts, or so easy as to require no effort at all. Double-translation is perhaps the best of all exercises for avoiding these extremes. It also possesses the invaluable advantage of being not less available in the first than in the last stage of study; for its difficulties may be diminished or increased at pleasure; and hence its perfect adaptation to public instruction, as the same task may be given in common to persons of very unequal proficiency who happen to be in the same class.

The choice of the model, especially in living languages, may always be suited to the capacity, progress, or requirements of the learner. In the commencement, the first version is made as literal as the genius of the national language permits; and the second translation is written shortly after the first, while the language of the original text is still vivid in his mind. A perusal of the text just before making the second translation, would also, if required, facilitate the reproduction. Moreover, the student can, at any moment, have recourse to it for the purpose of making sure of the words or construction which have escaped his memory. This reference to the model is, in many respects, preferable to using a dictionary.

As the student advances, he will, in his efforts to reproduce the text, rely more on his knowledge of the language and less on the recollection of the original. His first version, too, will be less and less literal; and he will gradually increase the interval between the two translations, thus leaving greater scope to memory and reflection. On the other hand, if he perseveres in the practice of the three other branches, simultaneously with this exercise, he will daily acquire greater facility in its execution.

In his first version the learner must be faithful to the original text, and, at the same time, conform to the genius of his own idiom: he should be careful neither to add to nor take from the ideas; for his business is rather to copy than to compose. It is often suggested, as a general direction, that the foreign work should be rendered in that style which, it may be presumed, its author would have employed had he written in the language into which the translation is made. This suggestion, although consistent with reason, must be received with some caution; for, if strictly followed, it may sometimes lead to mere imitation rather than to faithful interpretation of the original; besides, it may restrain the flexibility of the language and its adaptation to diversified expression of thought.

The correction of this translation has, in public instruction, great advantage over that of original essays: it can be effected simultaneously for all the members of a large class; and it occupies comparatively little time. Each learner having his version before him and pencil in hand, is, in turn, called upon to read a portion of the composition, on which the professor comments; the others, at the same time, marking such mistakes as they have made in common with the reader. The examination of an exercise of twenty lines, read aloud two or three times over, in portions of four or five lines, by a dozen learners, would amply suffice to elicit all the errors which may have been committed by fifty or more students. Essays, on the contrary, require each to be read through and examined separately; their correction, consequently, engaging the attention of only one learner at a time, leaves the others idle, and, from the time consumed, is impracticable in a class. Translation, by requiring all the learners to express the same ideas, brings their powers of composition to a closer and, hence, a more interesting contest; much useful information is also elicited by a critical examination of their different modes of expressing the same thoughts.

If the learner, having no competent person to whom he can submit his first version, wishes, nevertheless, to know whether it is correct, he may compare it with a good translation of his model. He might even make his second version from such a translation, if, from want of time, or any other reason, he wished to dispense with writing the first. This mode of proceeding is recommended by M. Guizot: "Take," he says, "a page translated from a good author into your own language or any other that you know; render this page in the language of the author, and compare your work with the original. By so doing, you learn the words, the syntax; and enter into the spirit of a language which is fixed in the memory by reading and writing." From this it is obvious that translations may always be turned to account, whether they accompany the original text or are published apart.

The second translation naturally presents more difficulty than the first, and cannot be made without the student constantly appealing to his recollection of the original text. These very efforts will have the effect of fixing in the memory its words and peculiar construction. The more idiomatic the foreign expressions, the greater must have been the effort to render them accurately, and the better will they be remembered.

Let it not be objected that learners would be apt to copy the original text, instead of performing the second translation. Such a practice is improbable at this advanced stage of the study and at the age we have assigned to them, especially if they are not unreasonably rebuked for the errors they commit. It rarely happens that young men betray the confidence placed in them. Under the worst circumstances, the second translation may be written in the presence of the instructor; or the text-book may be taken from them, when they are writing the second translation.

For greater convenience, the second version should be written in the same copybook opposite to the first, the alternate pages having been left blank for this purpose; thus comparison will be considerably facilitated.

The assistance of an instructor may be dispensed with for either the first or the second version, if the student has become familiar with the foreign language, and if, more especially, he can write his own correctly. The better he knows the latter the easier will he find this first operation. Even in case of his having followed our advice, and exercised himself more in direct reading than in translating, he will have no hesitation in rendering the ideas of the foreign text; for a person who can express his thoughts readily in the language into which he translates, will not require much previous practice in translation to succeed in this version. When he clearly conceives an idea, from whatever source derived, he will surely be able to express it.

In order to correct his second version, the student will compare it with the original, phrase for phrase, word for word, noting the differences he finds between the two; whether in orthography or phraseology, he will easily discover the reason of the preference to be given to the expressions of the original text, if he has read much, and bestowed some attention on grammar.

In case a student is as yet too young or too little versed in his own language to be able to account for the difference of words or construction, he will write the words of the model over his own, and will submit both to his instructor, who will find occasion in this parallel for entering into all the developments of literary criticism adapted to his age and proficiency.

According to the nature of the questions, the instructor will direct his pupil's attention to the orthography, the etymology, or the grammar; will point out the various shades of meaning in synonymes; and explain the difference between idiomatic and syntactic forms, between the literal and the figurative senses, between absolute and relative terms, between expressions of an elevated and those of a familiar style, as well as the various modes of expressing the same ideas, or the difference of idea resulting from difference of construction.

The doubts that each pupil of a class thus submits to the professor, will afford him an opportunity for giving instruction of the highest value to the whole class, and the more valuable as it is not to be found in the majority of the books usually put into the hands of young people.

It will sometimes happen that the student competes successfully with his model; for the same idea may be presented in different ways, and an author does not always choose the best. These little literary triumphs will greatly enhance the pleasure of the compositions and stimulate to perseverance.*

The moment when these comparisons are made is not the best time for the student to correct his exercise; he merely marks the errors with a pencil, reserving them for future correction from memory. The reflection required on a second consideration of the same subject to remember the differences previously noticed, will strengthen the memory and prevent the recurrence of the same errors. Reflecting on one's faults is the surest way of avoiding them in future.

If a person who learns a foreign language without a master, has recourse, for the double-translation, to a book with the two texts on oppo-

* It must not be supposed that we here flatter students at the expense of authors. The Vicar of Wakefield, for instance, which is frequently put into the hands of French pupils who are learning English, abounds with incorrect expressions.

site pages, he may, if necessary, compare his two versions with them; and if, for want of time, or any other reason, he cannot write the exercise, he will go through it orally, endeavoring to reproduce each text of the book, without looking at it first; and, as he advances with his version, he will compare it with the model text.

The choice of the text to be used as a model for double-translation, depends altogether on the kind of composition and style that is best suited to the learner's ultimate purpose. What most people want, however, is to be able to write letters, and this end can be best attained by the use of the class of books which we have recommended for initiating students in the first three arts. The familiarity of their subjects and the simplicity of their style are perfectly suited to the requirements of epistolary correspondence. It would be waste of time to attempt to rival the great writers.

If, when able to write well in prose, a student, endowed with a talent for poetry, should wish to try his hand at this sort of composition, or merely to study its mechanism, so as to better appreciate its merit, he will again have recourse to double-translation, taking for his model among the best poets, the one whose writings are the most congenial to his taste. The passages of poetry, read by the professor, as we have already suggested, having formed the student's ear to the rhythm and versification peculiar to the language which he studies, he will find little difficulty in reproducing them, if he is endowed with poetical discrimination.

The first version in prose, which affords him the occasion for transferring into his style some of the poetical beauties of his model, will not fail to extend his powers of composition in his own language, while the efforts he will make to reproduce in his second version the figurative language and the harmony of the style, will render him sensible of the difference between the literal and the figurative sense, between familiar and elevated expressions, between the style of prose and that of poetry. His vocabulary will also be enriched, owing to his being forced, by the necessity of rhyme, cadence, and measure, to examine many words which differ in termination, quantity, accent, or number of syllables, though nearly of the same meaning.

After having practised for some time on the ideas of good writers, endeavoring to imitate their forms of expression, the student may, with some chance of success, make an attempt at original composition. From the direct expression of thought by detached phrases, the transition is easy to a connected discourse. The words, having once become the direct and habitual signs of thought, will flow naturally from the pen, if the student exercises himself in the art of writing, as in the art of speaking, in treating subjects with which he has become familiar by reading and hearing.

In general, all interesting and well-written narratives, that have been read with this object in view, in the foreign language itself, will promote the student's progress by the impression which the direct reading will leave on the memory: both the form and the substance are thus equally retained. This practice in composition should also, at first, be combined with corresponding oral exercises, in such a manner that they mutually assist each other, either by the pupil's writing the narratives already made *vivâ voce*, or by relating to the professor those which have been written.

In proportion as the learner advances in composition, its difficulties should be increased by longer pieces, with a greater interval between the reading and the writing, until, at last, he can write without any preparation. For one who has stored his mind with various knowledge and cultivated his taste by the assiduous study of standard authors, the moment has come to rely solely on his own capabilities. He stands in precisely the same position with regard to the foreign language as to his own; and his improvement in both will be secured by the same means. He will devote his attention, according to circumstances, or the peculiar turn of his mind, to the epistolary style, to the relation of facts that have come to his knowledge, to the descriptions of objects, places, or persons, to summaries or analyses of his readings, or to any other subject on which he has clear and accurate notions.

When reading, hearing, phrase-making, and oral and written narration have, by the reiterated association of ideas with their signs, imparted the habit of thinking in the foreign tongue, as we think in our own, the one will not be more liable to be forgotten than the other. Both languages, equally making one with the thought, will adhere with the same tenacity to our individuality, and will be permanently assimilated with the elements of our intellectual constitution. The organs themselves through which this point is gained, the eye and ear, the instruments of curiosity, the tongue and hand, the instruments of imitation, contract habits corresponding to those of the faculties which direct their action.

The habits of language thus acquired will be infinitely more correct than those which an adult derives from a residence abroad. The student who follows our method, having only good models before him, either in his books or in his master, runs less risk of being misled than a person in a country the language of which he is yet unable to speak. Indeed, in this last case, being frequently thrown into the company of people who speak incorrectly, and being under the necessity of expressing his wants, of communicating his sentiments, before he has heard the words and phrases often enough to be able to reproduce them accurately, a person must make mistakes which, being seldom corrected, become habits never to be got rid of. As a compensation, however, he gains in facility what he loses in correctness.

Without unfolding the means by which a correct style is gained, as it is the very same which is required to attain a similar end in his own language, we will repeat our previous assertion that the art of writing well is the fruit of assiduous study of great writers, and of continuous efforts to imitate them, merely observing that it will be sufficient, in ordinary cases, to take for models texts in a simple and familiar style, as being the best suited for conversation and letter-writing.

Beyond this kind of composition we do not see any necessity for striving after a high degree of perfection in writing any language but one's own. The most eminent Latinists are not those who write their own language best: and never has the Latin versification of the colleges made a good English poet. The marked difference which characterizes the genius of languages will scarcely allow any one to write two in perfection. Such is the force of habit that if we express our thoughts in a foreign idiom, to the exclusion of our own, the forms peculiar to it will at times find their way into the latter, both in speaking and in writing. It is therefore advisable to restrict rather than to encourage composition in a foreign idiom.

In support of this truth we will quote Voltaire, who speaks from experience: "On my return from England," he says in a letter to Lord Bolingbroke, "when I had passed nearly two years in constant study of your language, I found myself embarrassed while composing a French tragedy. I had almost accustomed myself to think in English: I felt that the words of my own language no longer presented themselves to my imagination with the same abundance as before: it was like a stream, whose source had been turned aside; much time and effort were required to make it flow again in its original bed."

Grammar, rhetoric, and logic, will find their application as the complement of linguistic studies. To possess a critical acquaintance with a language, we must have studied its genius, have become thoroughly imbued with the principles which form its groundwork, and have analyzed expression in its relations with thought.

The exercises above recommended having their source in two powerful instincts, *curiosity and imitation*, and being, as reason prescribes, the actual practice of the arts to be acquired, success is infallible. They possess another great advantage, they are admirably adapted for public instruction, inasmuch as they afford to students of different degrees of proficiency the means of deriving equal benefit from the master's lessons, without loss of time for any of them. This advantage is especially owing to the fact that, as the pupils never perform in his presence the work they can do by themselves, he thus has time to teach them what they could not learn without his aid. Our method thus assigns to both pupils and master, their proper sphere of action. The former learn the written language, the latter teaches the spoken language.

This method dispenses with all the preparatory lessons, which only delay the practice of the language. Reading-books suffice for all the requirements of study. More than one volume at a time is never required for practising the different exercises it prescribes; and this is not one of its least advantages. A page, selected at random, in the first volume that comes to hand, offers the professor all the facilities for exercising his pupils in the practice of the four arts, for teaching them orthography, pronunciation, grammar, in short, every thing that relates to composition in the two languages.

It renders the learning of a language accessible to adults as well as to children, to the poor as well as to the rich, by supplying means of self-instruction, and requiring the help of a master only for the second half of the language, when the learner already knows the first and most important half.

Many persons actively engaged in business feel the want of knowing a foreign language, who are deterred from the attempt to learn it, on account of the tedious labor of the dictionary, and of all the drudgery imposed by routine as an indispensable preliminary. If the student, after spending much time on these unprofitable tasks, is compelled to discontinue them, he finds that he has learned nothing really useful, and retains only the painful recollection of the labor and fatigue he has gone through.

By following simple and natural processes in harmony with the end proposed, such as those we recommend, there can be no doubt that, in the maturity of reason, even at an advanced age, a person might, in six months, acquire what is useful in a living language, better than a boy of ten could do so in as many years, by the ordinary routine. The greatest linguists, from the Scaligers to Elihu Burritt, the learned blacksmith of Massachusetts, who is said to have learned above twenty languages, have nearly all acquired them in the maturity of life, and without masters, by following a method similar to the one we have sketched.

Plutarch, who began the study of Latin late in life, made rapid progress, because, as he himself says, his knowledge of things enabled him to enter into the thought of the writers. Themistocles, also advanced in years, learned Persian so well in one year, says his biographer, that he used to converse with the King of Persia on state affairs better than the Persians themselves. Cato the Censor learned Greek in his old age, and knew it thoroughly. Alfieri began the study of that language at forty-eight, and attained a high reputation as a Hellenist. Sir William Jones had passed his thirtieth year when he began to learn Eastern languages, in which he is known to have been deeply versed. Ogilby, the English translator of Virgil and Homer, had been a dancing-master; he did not know a word of Latin at forty, nor of Greek at fifty-four. Maugard, a distinguished man of letters, became, after three months of study, a successful teacher of Italian and Spanish, which he had learned in his sixtieth year. The celebrated Dr. Johnson undertook, when seventy years of age, the study of Dutch, with a view to test his capability to learn: the success of the experiment fully satisfied him that the powers of his mind were still unimpaired. Richard Cumberland, Bishop of Peterborough, at the age of eighty-three, learned the Coptic language, in order to read the Coptic New Testament, which Dr. Wilkins had just published.

It is fortunate for the perfectibility of man that the practical knowledge of languages is so easily acquired; for one of the principles of his nature, sociability, impels him instinctively to enter into communion with his fellow-creatures by the free manifestation of his thoughts. Whatever thwarts this instinct is an obstacle to his improvement.

Humanity is endowed with capacities which can be perfected only by the combination of minds: the whole mass is animated with a life which lies dormant in the isolated individual. A powerful impulse will therefore be given to the progress of civilization, by introducing into our schools and colleges a better system of linguistic teaching, which will bring nations into intellectual intercourse.

## CHAPTER VI.

### ON MENTAL CULTURE.

"L'étude des langues est beaucoup plus favorable aux progrès des facultés dans l'enfance que celle des mathématiques."

MADAME DE STAËL.

"The study of languages is much more favorable to the progress of the faculties in childhood than that of mathematics."

THERE are two distinct categories of students, those who learn a language for purely practical purposes, and those who learn it as a branch of education, either for the development of their mind, or as a means of extending their knowledge of the national idiom.

To the students of the first category, those whom an intellect, already ripe, inclines to a voluntary study, the *practical method*, as explained in the preceding pages, especially commends itself.

It is more especially profitable to those who, having completed their academical education, are preparing to embrace professions for which the knowledge of a foreign language is indispensable, and for those, whatever be their age, who, from taste or necessity, wish to enter on new fields of study, or to enlarge the circle of their social relations; but who, engaged in avocations which leave them little leisure, are averse to collateral studies, of which they do not see the necessity.

As regards the second category, including the youth of our colleges, more especially children under twelve or thirteen, the *comparative method* offers them all the means of attaining the end toward which their instructor ought to direct their attention, and which requires, on his part, a thorough knowledge of their language, as well as of the foreign idiom.

By oral instruction which bears on all the parts of the study, he will take an active part in all the exercises, which will become, under his direction, a real course of intellectual gymnastics. This is, for children, the most important part of scholastic education. They have abundance of time before them, and have no valid reasons for hurrying in the acquisition of a second language; for they would probably forget it, before they had occasion to use it.

The practical method, as it requires little mental effort, leads rapidly and exclusively to the mastery of a language; the comparative process, on the contrary, by presenting difficulties which unceasingly call the reflective powers into action, inures the learners to self-direction and intellectual labor, which constitute its chief merit as an instrument of moral and mental discipline, at the same time that it promotes advancement in the national language.

The first is best suited for modern languages, the second for the ancient.

The noble pages of history, eloquence, and poetry, which the dead languages exhibit, though few in number, will always stand as models of excellence. The beauties with which they abound cultivate and purify the taste, while reflection finds ample exercise in the consideration of thoughts and facts relating to an order of things above the homely realities of ordinary life.

Placed beyond the influence of caprice, the dead languages, so long as they are accepted as the groundwork of scholastic studies, and the test of excellence in literary composition, will tend to check the constant fluctuation of living languages. The Greek and Latin classics are in literature, what the works of the old masters are in painting. The love of novelty may for a time draw modern nations from the true principles of taste; the study of the immortal monuments of antiquity will always bring them back to the true standard.

Ancient languages must continue to occupy a large share of attention in the intellectual education of boys who are destined to pursuits which depend on literary acquirements. It is a narrow view to consider them as useful only to the learned professions. Acquaintance with them is beneficial not only to the clergyman, the physician, and the lawyer, but also to the archæologist, the philosopher, the man of letters, and the statesman, for they are the interpreters of ancient monuments, the original receptacles of our laws, the source of our modern dialects, forming a bond which unites European nations with one another, and with antiquity. Their study involves that intellectual discipline which gives the greatest possible development to the faculties of man, and is the common ground on which the noblest intellects are brought into contact.

Mathematics, far from being, as commonly believed, the best logical exercise, would, if studied exclusively, rather tend to disqualify the mind for general reasoning. They confine the student to a narrower circle of mental exercises than languages and philosophy; they habituate him to a routine of argumentation which presents little variety; they awaken his judgment to the relation of quantity, but, neglecting quality and all other important relations, they leave in abeyance the powers of the understanding which are most useful in the ordinary circumstances of life.

In the study of languages the mind is engaged as in the world; it is formed to all modes of reasoning, to all kinds of argumentation, by the reading and hearing of serious subjects. The reading of good books is a practical logic in the exercises intended to teach speaking and writing; we find the same dealings with words and ideas as in social intercourse, the same caution and discrimination between rules and exceptions, the same exercises of conception, imitation, and invention; finally, the same methods of induction, analogy, and analysis.

At every step in mathematical demonstrations there is a constant perspicuity, a straight and limited path marked out, from which it is almost impossible to wander. But in the expression of thought, and in literary investigations, the learner has to feel his way, reflect, compare, judge, apply his own experience, weigh probabilities, disentangle networks of inconsistencies, and lay bare sophistical plausibilities. In this necessity for a diversified and complicated action of the reasoning powers consists the chief value of classical and literary studies.

The learning of languages embraces thought and its expression. The operations of the mind may indeed be said to be identical with the use of language. The various acquirements which constitute the complete possession of a foreign idiom afford, through the exercises indispensable for their attainment, the means of cultivating attention and raising the intellectual powers from their original state to the highest degree of improvement. The mental discipline generated by a rational method begins with those mysterious lessons by which the learner associates signs with ideas, and continues through the whole course of the study, by means of critical explanations, translation, reading of foreign works, and analysis of their style. The disclosure of the thoughts and sentiments of good writers will gratify his curiosity, excite his sympathies, improve his taste, invigorate his judgment, enrich his memory, and enlarge his understanding.

The continual comparison of two idioms which results from one being acquired through the other, keeps observation and reflection constantly on the alert. But, as we can compare only such things as we know, the comparative method will not produce all its fruits, unless we possess the art of reading the foreign language. Then only shall we be able to establish, with regard to thought and style, an interesting and profitable parallel between the native and the foreign writers. We therefore cannot acquire that art too soon in the ancient as well as in the modern languages.

To advance safely in reading, children as yet incapable of self-direction, should be assisted in all the investigations to which translation leads. They will be told the true meaning of idioms, the different acceptations of words, and the difference of import between those called synonymes. They will be assisted in rendering faithfully the original text, and in rendering it conformably to the genius of their own tongue. By exercising them in comparing this text with the interpretation which accompanies it, the professor will clear up their doubts, explain irregularities, and enable them to overcome all the difficulties that are presented by the difference of construction in the two languages.

As the dead languages are no longer used for the oral exchange of thought, the speaking exercises will be set aside, which will allow more time to be devoted to the explanation and translation of authors. This branch of the study assumes an importance which it cannot have in living languages, and which will prove all the more profitable to the pupils in proportion to the skill of their instructor in their native tongue, and to the extent and soundness of his information.

If translation is objectionable as a means of understanding the foreign text, it is otherwise, when considered as an exercise, either in oral or written composition: it then becomes a powerful auxiliary for improving a learner in his native idiom, and for exercising him in improvisation, from the moment he possesses the art of reading the foreign language. He thus increases his native vocabulary by the use of words which were not previously familiar to him.

Aided by careful study of national writers and

orators, oral translation at sight, if continued for some time, will prove a better preparation than rules for acquiring that magic power—extempore speaking—which instantaneously calls up the most appropriate terms, and suits the form of expression to the idea.

Written translation is preferable to oral for forming a good style, and acquiring great powers of expression in the national language; for the necessity of reading on, in order to grasp the subject, does not allow time to polish our phraseology, or to seek the forms of speech which best conform to the genius of our language. In the first version of the double-translation, we practise the art of writing under favorable conditions; because we can then bestow on the work all the reflection required for the choice of words, their idiomatic arrangements, and the logical connection of ideas.

"It is by translating," says De Gérando, "that young people learn best all the laws of the art of writing." D'Alembert also says: "If you wish to be one day translated, begin yourself by translating. The work of translation will yield a rich harvest of principles and ideas, and prove an excellent school in the art of writing."

He who attempts composition without first laying in a large provision of knowledge, will at best deal out none but commonplace ideas, and conceal poverty of thought under pomp of phraseology. But a second language presents an inexhaustible source of interesting compositions, which, while they serve as models for the manner of treating a subject, afford by translation the best means of practising the art of writing.

In translating from a standard work a learner habituates himself to express sound ideas: he is thereby led to reflect on subjects which he had not previously considered, and his sphere of thought is enlarged, as is also his power of expression; for it is more difficult to render the ideas of others than one's own. In original essays a learner is not always completely master of his subject, and is apt sometimes to modify the ideas as they arise in the mind to suit them to his scanty stock of words. Translation, by binding him to the particular ideas of the author, teaches him to overcome difficulties; original composition, by leaving him the option both of the substance and the form, only teaches him to avoid them. At a later period, he will experience no difficulty in expressing his own ideas in the native idiom, when he is able to render accurately those of the great writers of another language.

With these models before him, the professor can, without difficulty, familiarize his pupils with all that gives precision, force, elegance, and harmony to composition, with all that can improve their taste or exercise their judgment. "It is necessary," says Lord Brougham, "to acquire correct habits of composition in our own language, first by studying the best writers, and next by translating copiously into it . . . . A man will speak well in proportion as he has written much." Cicero tells us that he owed his success as a public speaker to his having translated much from the Greek orators.

Translation, in addition to its special merit as a means of extending the power of expression, presents advantages as an intellectual exercise, that are not to be obtained from writing in a language that is as yet but little known. Ascertaining the precise meaning of a foreign author, and selecting the words and forms of speech in the native tongue which most exactly convey his thoughts, are double operations eminently adapted to discipline the mind. Before the learner ventures to translate the foreign text, he must have fully apprehended the ideas of the author and have made them his own, by going with him over the same fields of investigation. It is only when he has a clear conception of them that he can at all think of giving expression to them.

This second operation again brings into action his mental powers and all his resources of language: he is led to examine why one term has been selected in preference to another, to distinguish what propositions are principal, what secondary, and to ascertain what is their mutual dependence. As almost every word may be translated in different ways, and every sentence in different styles, his discrimination and sagacity are constantly exercised in selecting the native expressions most suitable in each particular case. He must exert his imagination and judgment not to overcharge his author's meaning, nor to fall short of it; he must be well imbued with the peculiar energy and grace of his model, to be able to transfuse the same qualities into his own style; and whether he succeed or fail, the actual labor of the attempt will be beneficial to him.

In the efforts made by the translator to render the original text clearly and idiomatically, he corrects, analyzes, compares, and harmonizes his phrases. Thus he observes, reflects, judges: in one word, he learns to think.

Translation, to be of any benefit to learners as yet little versed in their own language, must be made under the master's guidance: he will direct them in the choice of words, the use of figures, the harmonious arrangement of periods, and all the elements of a good style. For this purpose he must himself possess an accurate and extensive knowledge of his pupils' language. Persevering in oral translation under the direction of an enlightened instructor would be more generally useful to young people than aiming at direct reading, an exercise tending exclusively to forwarding them in the foreign language. Improvement in the national idiom, for which the study of a second language is so desirable, must always be kept in view. Classical instruction is most favorable to the attainment of this object: hence, every lesson in Greek or Latin should be made a lesson in English.

In ordinary circumstances, the classical professor, who is necessarily much better acquainted with the language of his pupils, which is his own, than with the Latin and Greek which he teaches, can make the latter subservient to their improvement in the vernacular more effectually than could be done through living idioms by foreigners, who are seldom well versed in that language. A great difference, therefore, arises in the mode of proceeding: the study of the ancient languages is essentially a means of extending one's knowledge of his own language; but since little assistance can be obtained from foreign teachers toward any considerable advancement in the latter, an extensive acquaintance with it becomes indispensable as a groundwork for mastering a foreign living language. The ends to be attained by studying these two categories of languages differ essentially: the dead languages are learned for the sake of the national idiom, the living languages for their own sake. These, as necessary vehicles of thought, require the ideas to be directly associated with the words, a process unsuited to the dead languages, which prove beneficial to learners only by being studied through the native tongue. The practical and the comparative methods cannot be followed simultaneously. The adoption of one implies the rejection of the other.

Those innovators accordingly commit an egregious blunder, who propose to substitute the modern for the ancient languages in the instruction of youth. Although English, French, Italian, and German, may fairly compete with the latter in force, lucidity, and gracefulness of expression, at the same time that they far surpass them in the number and importance of the benefits which they confer through life on their votaries, still they can never supersede them. But, were such a change to take place, foreigners, who would consequently become the most competent professors in what would then be the chief department of collegiate instruction and the best judges of literary merit, must be placed at the head of academical establishments, and invested with the highest university honors. This would be a complete anomaly, a state of things altogether incompatible with the existing form of literary institutions and repugnant to national feelings.

The practice of writing the dead languages should be indulged in very sparingly in public instruction, the more so as it consumes a considerable portion of time, and thus unreasonably and unprofitably lengthens the period of classical studies. The attention of learners ought to be confined to what is really useful in these studies, namely, the reading and analysis of the great writers of antiquity. It is by reflecting on their thoughts and their style; it is especially by transferring, through translation or imitation, their beauties into the national idiom, and not by caricaturing them in their own, that classical instruction may be productive of real advantage, that the understanding may be exercised, and a command of the native tongue secured.

Depth of learning in ancient literature is far from being the test of excellence in the national language. In a rational course of instruction the national classics should be studied as much as those of antiquity. To know Latin and Greek is a great intellectual luxury, but to know one's own language is an intellectual necessity.

In the instruction of youth the national tongue should hold a preëminence, which, until now, has been denied to it; for it is more particularly the instrument of the mind's operations, the record of its stores, the manifestation of our feelings, our affections, our intellectuality. Its writers and orators, its genius and resources, should, among a people careful of their own dignity, occupy young persons from the earliest to the latest period of scholastic instruction. It is in that tongue that they should be taught to think, to speak, and to write. To it belongs by right the prize of excellence adjudged by the old universities to the Latin tongue. It should be considered more honorable, as it is more consistent and more useful, to speak and write English like the best English and American speakers and writers, than Latin like Cicero and Tacitus.

In the private affairs of life, as in political or international questions, he who speaks or writes the best will always gain an ascendency over his fellow-citizens. Speech is power. The great end of classical and literary education ought to be to confer this power, the most useful, the most delightful, the most admirable of human acquirements.

An enlightened American teaching a foreign living language, which he only knows how to read, would still have a noble task before him, if he endeavored, through translation, to improve his pupils in their own idiom. He would be able, better than a foreigner, to ascertain, by their manner of translating, whether they really understand their author.

Direct reading and hearing will, also, like translating, aid in cultivating in youth the two-fold talent of speaking and composing in the national language, if the professor makes them repeat *vivâ voce* or in writing what they have read or heard in the foreign idiom. This exercise will not only test their diligence, but will also, under his direction, be the means of acquiring a ready delivery and great power of expression. On the other hand, under the expectation that they will have to give an account of what they read or hear, they will read and listen more carefully, and will thus more firmly impress on their minds the subjects brought under their notice.

Narration exercises the intellectual memory, that which proceeds from understanding the subject and rests on the connection of the ideas, on the relation of cause and effect, and on that of premises and consequences. This noble faculty plays a far higher part in our mental organization than mechanical memory, or recollection of words by their accidental collocation, which, having nothing to do with the judgment, consists in retaining and repeating words in a given order, rather than in recalling ideas by their logical concatenation.

In written as well as in oral compositions founded on imitation, the powers of observation, reflection, and judgment, are constantly brought into activity by the necessity of studying models, comparing them with their copies, and discriminating between different forms of expression and the different ways of treating a subject.

In original compositions, those of a purely narrative character, resting on the chain of incidents, exercise more especially memory and imagination; whereas, descriptions and dissertations, without rejecting the aid of these two faculties, call for higher intellectual powers: the first requires accurate investigation of things and nice discrimination in classifying the subject; the second depends chiefly on a clear understanding and strict attention to logical relations. The more minute the description and the more philosophical the dissertation, the greater will be the demand on the reflective and the reasoning powers.

The double-translation, by placing in juxtaposition the genius of two languages and of two nations, affords the professor a favorable opportunity for enlightening his pupils on points of great interest, arising from the resemblances and differences which are rendered obvious by this twofold operation.

The resemblances between two languages establish the principles which constitute general or comparative grammar; the differences between them mark out the rules of the particular grammar of each. The comparison of several languages, with a view to ascertain their lexicographic and grammatical affinities, throws light on their affiliation, on the migration of nations, and on the history of man. The professor, without touching on considerations above the reach of his pupils, will sometimes speak on these subjects, point out the origin of words and trace the modifications which they have undergone in passing from one language to another.

If general grammar be properly explained to young persons, at a time when the mind is capable of such a study, there cannot be a doubt that it will open before them a large field on which they may exercise their reasoning faculties. Rising, therefore, with them above the facts, the generalization of which constitutes *the art* of grammar, the professor will easily enter on the consideration of the universal laws which govern languages and constitute *the science* of grammar.

This high branch of literature is too much neglected in scholastic instruction. Boys are made to learn Latin, Greek, French, and German grammars, but are seldom taught the laws which are common to all languages, in contradistinction from those which are peculiar to each.

The foreigner, who is not competent to give this higher kind of instruction, and cannot improve his pupils in their own language, from not knowing it thoroughly, should confine himself to his special sphere, and follow the processes which we have above described, in order to give them a practical knowledge of his own language, so as to make it for them an instrument of thought.

If, however, he is versed in the grammar of his own language and in literary criticism, let him occasionally take up one of the standard works which his class have read, and, after having ascertained that it is perfectly understood, let him make them analyze it as regards the words, their nature, inflections, roots, pronunciation, derivation, synonymy, and different acceptations; let him assist them in inferring the rules of grammar, from the recurrence of the same forms of expression. He will afterward, at a more advanced stage, turn their attention to style, point out the force and propriety of terms, the precision, elegance, and harmony of periods, every thing, in short, which constitutes literary merit.

Let the professor guard against the degenerating of these considerations into mere parsing, an exercise which occupies so considerable a place in public instruction, and which, confined, as it usually is, to merely technical terms, aids in no way to the cultivation of the mind, or to the practical acquaintance with a language.

Particular grammar is an inductive art; and, in all such arts, we arrive at principles from facts: the more numerous these are, the more general the rules. Custom is the law of language, grammar is only its generalization. Thus is grammar made, and thus it must be learned, from the language; not the language from the grammar.

All the rules of grammar are in the written page; it is the teacher's office to bring them out, carefully avoiding abstract formulas, which children understand so imperfectly and forget so easily. If the latter had previously learned the rules, they would be deprived of the exercise in observation, comparison, analogy, and generalization, to which reasoning by induction leads. Moreover, rules which apply to unknown facts, are pure abstractions devoid of interest; whereas, the mind delights in classifying scattered notions, and discovering the reason of known facts.

This inductive or analytical mode of studying grammar, similar to the intellectual process by which we arrive at a knowledge of natural laws, is the most rational and the most favorable to mental discipline: it consists in observing facts, comparing them, remarking their resemblances and differences, and afterward bringing into the same class all similar facts. Those which may be generalized constitute the rules, and those which are not comprised within any class form the exceptions.

The exercise of phrase-making, more especially by multiplying the expression of thought, aids in giving a practical knowledge of grammar. The construction of phrases after a model is the application of syntax to the expression of thought, for there is no phrase which does not exemplify some rule of syntax. It may be made by a judicious instructor the source of much grammatical information to his pupils. In classifying and generalizing constructions, formed on a principle of analogy, the laws which govern them are naturally evolved by induction. Practice and theory mutually aid each other, and grammar is thus learned, not by an act of the memory, but by an act of judgment.

Beneficial as these grammatical inductions may be to a learner, he should not be refused the instrument which may help him in his observations. It is not enough that he should infer the rules of composition from the phraseology: this incidental way of learning the grammatical principles of a language would never give him a complete and systematic knowledge of them. A good treatise on the subject is indispensable, if he wishes to have a comprehensive view of the theory. A few months assiduously devoted to this study would suffice to methodize and complete the scattered notions of grammar, acquired by induction; and, if he aspires to being a grammarian, he should take up different treatises on the subject, read, compare, and judge for himself.

A familiarity with the national grammar will be the best preparation for a similar study in the foreign language, as the learner will find in the grammar of that language the same technical denominations, and the same definitions. It renders more intelligible the explanations of the professor, who is often obliged, even at the outset, to advert to grammatical distinctions.

It also assists in translating from the native into the foreign tongue, because, in order to ascertain what is the foreign expression corresponding to the native, one must know the nature of the words to be translated and their functions in the sentence. On a clear conception, for example, of the person, tense, and mood of the English verb depends the correctness of the foreign one. If the learner has to render in French that part of an English verb which ends in *ed*, he must be able to distinguish, in every case, whether that verb is in the preterite or past participle, since it is differently translated, according as it is one or the other. Again, if *but* be the word to be rendered into French, he must discriminate what part of speech it is in each particular instance; that is, what is its precise import; because, in its triple office of an adverb, a preposition, and a conjunction, it admits of different translations, viz., *ne que*, *excepté*, *mais*.

In addition to words belonging to different classes, there are a great many which admit of various equivalents in other languages, according as they are used in a literal or a figurative sense. As a general rule, a word is interpreted in another language in as many ways as it admits of different significations.

Although deficiencies and irregularities abound in all languages, they seldom occur on the same occasions in any two of them. No phrase is rendered literally, the constituent parts of which are, in their arrangement, relations, or meanings, inconsistent with the idea expressed, or with the laws of language, as, for example, the following idioms: He was offered a situation (familiarly used for *a situation was offered to him*). How do you like the book? (the word *how* signifying in what manner, and the whole phrase implying that the person questioned does like the book, constitute a double inconsistency with the idea meant to be conveyed). I wish I was there now (a past tense used to mark the present). To wait on, to call upon, to hear from a person (three verbs used anomalously).

From these observations, it is obvious that a thorough knowledge of the national idiom must be a great help toward acquiring a foreign living tongue. But classical education, which, as was seen, is intended not so much to teach a second language as to improve young people in their own, does not require any extensive knowledge of the latter as a preparation: this education, on the contrary, secures it, under the direction of an able instructor. With his assistance all grammatical irregularities in the vernacular, all anomalies which might otherwise escape notice, are elicited by submitting them to the analytical process of translation: and the learner, being thus led to inquire what are the different ideas attached to the same words, and what native expressions do or do not conform either to the idea intended or to the general principles of grammar, acquires a habit of nice discrimination and a critical knowledge of his own idiom.

Under any circumstances, the usual order of study should be altered: the foreign grammar must be transferred from the lower to the higher classes, while the national should be taught as a foundation for linguistic studies; the lower classes might continue to be denominated the grammar classes.

Grammatical studies, although they do not necessarily impart the power of expression so effectually as the imitation of the great models, furnish the student with the means of entering into the secrets of composition, of exploring the mysterious laws of creative genius, and of submitting his own productions to the control of reason and of established principles. It is then that theory becomes a useful auxiliary to practice.

When the learners have completely mastered the art of hearing, the professor should occasionally address them in the foreign language on various subjects of instruction. These subjects should be selected in reference to the studies in which they are engaged at the time, and more particularly to the higher departments of that language; he may treat of its genius and comparative merit; investigate its origin, rise, and progress; unfold its importance as a vehicle of thought, or as a store of information; comment critically on its best works, and examine its literature, considered either absolutely or relatively to the national literature of his pupils. Should he feel diffident in extemporaneous delivery, he may read to them from the most eminent writers in the foreign language passages which would enrich their minds with useful knowledge and familiarize them with a pure and elegant style.

In reading the Greek or Latin poets to his advanced pupils, the professor should avail himself of the superiority of ancient prosody, to point out the effects of contrasted sounds, of long and short, high and low notes; he should explain to them the principles of quantity, accents, cadences, cæsuras, rhythms, metres, pauses, all that constitutes the mechanism of verse and the melody of language.

We have seen that there are three modes of proceeding in learning languages: 1. The exclusively practical method, that of the mother tongue. 2. The exclusively comparative method, that which suits the study of Greek and Latin. 3. The practico-comparative, that which is required for foreign living languages. The direct association of ideas with their signs is the essence of the first. Translation from either language into the other is the essence of the second. By the third, the learner passes from comparison to practice, from the indirect to the direct use of the language.

Although the comparative method can never completely secure the full mastery of a language, it will nevertheless remain the privilege of classical instruction. It is the only one which permits an enlightened professor to give his pupils the greatest benefit of his own acquirements and his superior knowledge of their language. As for the practico-comparative method, while it shares in the benefits of the other two, its special office is to make the foreign language available for the exchange of ideas: it adds little to man's intellectual power.

Classical learning, as the most important in the education of youth, claims the larger portion of the time apportioned to literary studies. With regard to modern languages, if their study is commenced at a suitable age, eighteen months or two years at the utmost would suffice for gaining that practical acquaintance with one, which would enable a student to read it with pleasure and converse in it with ease.

## CHAPTER VII.

### ON ROUTINE.

"Gardez-vous de la routine, c'est la mort de l'enseignement."

MATTER.

"Beware of routine, it is fatal to teaching."

A METHOD, in order to be rational and efficient, must be consistent with the end proposed. We learn a foreign language for the sake of making it the instrument of thought in the international exchange of ideas; but, of the four arts by which this exchange is effected, the first two are indisputably of far higher importance and more general application than the other two, both as an end and as a means. The method ought then, first, to teach these two arts. Yet, strange to say, people will persist in saying that the principal object in studying a foreign living language is to learn to speak it; forgetting, moreover, that it must be understood before it is spoken, and that, to write well, one must have read much.

This popular error has given birth to nearly

all the methods in vogue. For the most part they aim at the rapid acquirement of that art, and of that alone. Contemning the order and wise slowness of nature, they break off the chain which connects together the four great objects of a language, neglect the most useful part of intellectual communication, and necessarily resort to processes, which are at war with the fundamental principles of language, the laws of our mental organization, and the requirements of social intercourse. We need not be surprised, therefore, at the almost universal failure of linguistic teaching.

Grammar, exercises, reading aloud, mnemonic lessons of words, dialogues, extracts from authors, and other processes established by routine chiefly for speaking a foreign language, fail even in this object; for imitation, by which alone this art can be acquired, is altogether set aside. These preliminary exercises, from the importance often attached to them, and the time they consume, sacrifice the end to the means, and lengthen unreasonably the study of languages. They cannot, therefore, enter into a rational system of teaching.

Of all the dilatory means which tradition and routine have introduced into the teaching of languages, grammar has perhaps been the greatest obstacle to their attainment. By a deplorable violation of the laws of nature, the rule is considered as essential, the example as secondary, and grammar is made the basis of the study.

The art of grammar adds little to the learner's vocabulary, and yet an extensive stock of words is the most indispensable acquisition for good speaking and good writing; because, without copiousness of language, there is no possibility of suiting expressions to ideas in the diversified circumstances of intellectual communication. It does not guide in the choice of words, nor tell their orthography, pronunciation, or accentuation. It affords no assistance in ascertaining when the two languages differ in the application of apparently corresponding words, in the use of prepositions, in the genders or numbers of nouns, or in the mode of supplying ellipses and the deficiencies of a language. It does not teach the propriety of metaphors, the euphony of periods, the idiomatic forms of speech, the various acceptations of words, the different shades of meaning which characterize synonymes; in fine, none of those niceties of expression which constitute the genius, force, and elegance of a language, and which can be acquired only through an extensive and critical reading of standard works.

Grammar, then, is not *the art* of speaking and writing correctly. All that can be said of it is that it contributes, within certain limits, to correct speaking and writing, but is insufficient, of itself, to attain that end. Authors of grammars who devote all their time and attention to the rules of a language, are rarely distinguished either as speakers or writers.

Voltaire, who, like all great writers, gained his literary eminence without having devoted much of his time to grammar, warns us against the perusal of most grammars, and especially of that of Girard, which is, however, one of the best in the French language. "It would serve," he says, "to corrupt the style of the reader." "We are amazed at the weakness of the human mind," says Count de Gébelin, "when we consider the oversights and blunders which are committed by the ablest grammarians."

Grammar assists so little in freeing the expression of thought from inaccuracy, obscurity, and nonsense, that a composition may be strictly grammatical, and withal replete with incongruities of all sorts, bad spelling, inappropriate terms, vulgarisms, cacophonies, amphibologies, pleonasms, barbarisms, unsuitable figures, illogical deductions. Every day we hear the most erroneous expressions used by foreigners, while they strictly follow the rules of grammar, which, there is every reason to believe, must have chiefly engaged their attention in studying English.

But, absurd as it is to take to the letter the definition usually given of grammar, it is more absurd still to make it the first step in linguistic studies; since, as we have shown, it affords no aid toward understanding either the written or the spoken language. One might be able to repeat a grammar from beginning to end, without being a whit the more capable of understanding or speaking two words in the language. Grammar does not impart the power of speaking to him who has not the materials of expression.

Admitting even that it teaches to speak and write correctly, it must not be inferred that it teaches to speak and write, but only to do so correctly; in other words, to avoid or correct errors in the expression of thought. A person must therefore begin to speak and write, before he can derive any advantage from rules. "The grammar of a language," says Sicard, "cannot be learned before one is able to speak it." "To begin with learning rules is a gross error" (Condillac). "I would fain have any one name to me that tongue, which any one can learn, or speak as he should do, by the rules of grammar" (Locke). "An age of theory, of pure theory, would not advance a person one step in the knowledge of a language; it would not teach to translate a phrase" (Lemare). "The rules of grammar which are results, demonstrated for him who already knows the languages, and has made them a subject of meditation, cannot, in any way, be the means of knowing them, for him who is not acquainted with them. They are consequences; we cannot, without doing violence to reason, present them to him as principles" (Talleyrand). "May the child," exclaims Pluche, "long remain ignorant that there are in the world such things as grammars!"

Can grammar be considered as a safe and intelligible guide, when the grammarians themselves are but indifferent speakers and writers? Their definitions and rules are for the most part obscure, incomplete, and erroneous. Moreover, the diversity of opinion which exists between them, at once shows the difficulty of the subject and the absence of clear notions on the theory of grammar. In the whole circle of the arts and sciences there is not one in which the definitions and classifications of their different authors are more discordant and more uncertain. The most elementary questions have not yet received solutions which place them in the number of universally admitted truths. "Grammatici certant et sub judice lis est" (Quintillian).

Those who express themselves best in their own language owe their superiority far more to their own reflections than to the precepts of grammarians. There was no methodical treatise on grammar at the time when Shakespeare, Milton, Dryden, Addison, Pope, Johnson, formed their style in writing. The same remark holds good with regard to Cicero, Virgil, Horace, to Molière, Pascal, Corneille, La Fontaine, Boileau, Racine, to Dante, Petrarch, Boccaccio, and many other celebrated writers, who, so far from having learned any thing from grammarians, supplied them with the materials from which they inferred their rules.

One of the greatest mistakes arising from the false definition of grammar, a mistake against which the public cannot be too much on its guard, is that committed by certain persons who, knowing only the grammar of a foreign language, set up as professors of the latter, under the pretence that teaching the grammar is teaching the language itself. Many compilers of grammars for beginners put forth similar pretensions, as is obvious from their giving such books the title of "Method," for teaching, etc. (the language of which they treat).

It frequently happens that grammar is not taught, but imposed as a lesson to be learned by rote, on young children incapable of understanding it. The verbatim repetition of the text is even sometimes insisted upon, so that, under this implicit injunction to attend to words rather than to sense, they seldom make an effort to comprehend what they learn. "Nothing," says Condillac, "is more useless than to weary a child by loading his memory with the rules of a language which he does not understand. Of what use is it for him to know rules by heart, if it is not in his power to apply them?"

No set of rules committed to memory will either form a profound scholar, or, what is infinitely more important, create habits of patient observation and judgment. A man might be acquainted with the results of many profound inquiries in all the various sciences; he might take them on credit, and act as if he believed them to be true; but his understanding would not be one jot advanced above that of an uninstructed workman. If the knowledge of all facts and the conclusions of all researches could be poured into a man's mind without his own labor, he would really be less wise than he who has been properly trained to work the rule of simple proportion.

It is not the letter, but the spirit of the rule, which can be productive of benefit. In grammar, as in morals and the sciences, it is impossible to apply a rule or to reason from a principle, unless we enter into the spirit of it. The most accurate rule, the wisest precept, if accepted without being understood in all its bearings, can never be applied with perfect fitness in all possible circumstances; it will even become a continual source of errors.

Let us, then, hope that we shall soon see banished, from every school, "a method which," as De Gérando observes, "is in direct opposition to the nature of things, which besets with abstractions the novitiate of a mind as yet unprepared for them, and which enters upon the study of a language, by the very notions which the knowledge of that language alone can give."

All the objections to grammar for beginners apply equally to the written exercises, their usual auxiliaries. They cannot, any more than grammar, facilitate the apprenticeship to reading, for the understanding of a written text does not in any way imply the power of writing. Common sense requires that the learner should read before he writes, so as to know what is the best usage, in order to conform to it.

It is, besides, contrary to reason to force children to compose in an idiom in which they will perhaps never have occasion to write, when they make comparatively so few efforts to acquire this same talent in their own, which would be so useful in the course of life, and so favorable to intellectual culture.

The intimate relations between the thought and the style render composition a highly intellectual exercise, only when the language is for the writer the direct and spontaneous expression of his ideas, and when he is practically conversant with its genius and phraseology, as is the case with the vernacular. But the learner who translates into a foreign idiom not yet familiar to him, does not think in it, and is even unable to choose the words which would best convey his ideas, because he knows not their true import, nor the various shades of meaning which they convey; his consideration of words does not go beyond their orthography, their concord, or their respective places, according as he is directed by the rules, which he has previously learned, or has before his eyes—a purely mechanical process, not much above a culinary operation from a cookery-book.

These premature attempts at writing, as they do not permit him to exercise his imitative or imaginative powers, and fraught with errors as they must be, are calculated to vitiate rather than improve his taste. It is utterly impossible, as it has been erroneously believed, that they should cultivate his understanding, or impart to him the power of discovering and appreciating the beauties of foreign literary productions. They seem, like most other contrivances of routine, to have been introduced, in order to afford the instructor an opportunity of correcting errors which could be avoided by processes more conformable to reason.

They are condemned by all all writers who have treated of linguistic studies. Rollin, timid as he was in his educational reforms, says: "To write Latin well, one must know the turns, the idioms, the rules of the language, and have at command a considerable provision of words, the force of which is felt, and the just application of which can be made. Now, all this can be done only by explaining authors, who are like a living dictionary and a speaking grammar, in which are learned by experience the force and the true use of words and phrases, as well as the rules of syntax. I have no hesitation in declaring that, in the beginning, written exercises in the foreign tongue ought to be entirely excluded, as being calculated only to torment young people by painful and useless labor, and to inspire them with dislike to a study which generally draws on them nothing but reprimands and punishments."

Unwilling to swell this volume with quotations, we will be content with naming, among those who condemn the practice, Roger Ascham, Milton, Locke, the distinguished scholars of Port Royal, Montaigne, Dumarsais, Pluche, Radonvilliers, La Châlotais, Diderot, D'Alembert, J. J. Rousseau, Bernardin de St. Pierre, Guizot.

Some partisans of routine, unwilling to reject the method of grammatical exercises, although aware of its defects, have compiled manuals, in which they contrive every possible means to facilitate the observance of the rules and spare young people the trouble of reflecting: they give not only the foreign words, but their order; they indicate the gender and number, mood and tense; they point out when words ure to be omitted or supplied. Learners mechanically avail themselves of this assistance without inquiring into the difference of the idiom between the two languages, often even without reading the rule before they write the exercise, and without attending to the idea to be expressed; so that the remedy is worse than the evil. Never have these unconnected compositions led to the formation of a good style.

Inappropriate and inefficient as are grammatical exercises for acquiring the art of composition in a foreign language, they are, in absurdity, far surpassed by the practice of translating into it from a national author at an early period of the study, when the learner has no rules, no model to guide him; when he knows neither the different acceptations of the foreign words nor the shades of difference between synonymes; when he cannot even imagine whether that language admits, or does not admit, of rendering literally the forms of another; whether it has or has not equivalent idiomatic or figurative expressions. It is so preposterous, that it defies all argumentation. Even at an advanced period, it is a most injudicious practice. To translate into the native idiom, presents, as has been seen, great obstacles to those most conversant with it; how, in the name of common sense, can it be done in a language with which one is not acquainted? It is an absurdity of the same kind as that of reading aloud before having heard the words.

The cause of this anomaly may be found in the fact that foreigners who teach their own language, being at first little versed in that of their pupils, feel their inability to translate into it, and resort to the opposite practice. Their correction of compositions in their own language gives an appearance of usefulness to their services; but, in reality, they only delay the progress of their pupils, in the first three arts, without teaching them the fourth. Whether from pride or weakness of mind, men seldom think of leaving off a false course on which they have entered.

They fall into error through ignorance; they remain in it from habit.

The time which the unfortunate victims of routine spend at this work in the absence of the instructor, leaves them but little leisure for reading; and, on the other hand, the correcting of the tasks in class takes up a considerable portion of the master's time, which would be much better employed in explaining to them the ancient classics, or in enabling them to understand oral expression in living languages. They read, in the intervals of their lessons, only as much as their instructor has time to hear them translate in class, which is far from being sufficient for acquiring the art of reading or becoming acquainted with all the forms of the written language, and especially with its orthography.

Learners, not obtaining from example any assistance toward acquiring this elementary department of composition, are made to resort to special exercises, more or less irrational, as they reject the commands of nature. Among others, we may mention dictation, a practice altogether inefficient. In Italian and Spanish, for instance, the conformity of the spelling with the pronunciation renders it utterly useless. So uniform is the representative power of the letters in these languages, that to pronounce an Italian or a Spanish word is to spell it. In German, dictation is not much more useful, because the same letters representing the same sounds and articulations, it suffices to know the power of their alphabetical characters, in order to deduce the spelling of the words from their sounds. French orthography, which is in frequent disagreement with its pronunciation, should be learned by a reference to its orthoëpy, etymology, and syntax, rather than by dictation. As for the English language, which is rarely spelt as it is pronounced, its orthography is the fruit of practice alone. He who knows the spelling of an English word derives no benefit from writing it, and he who is not previously acquainted with it, will seldom be able to spell it from hearing.

Dictation, like reading aloud, is a test of proficiency, not a means of teaching. Although, however, it cannot prevent the commission of errors, it affords the means of detecting and correcting them. But, viewed even in this light, dictation should be resorted to cautiously; because, for one word that the pupil may thus learn to spell, he wastes time in writing many which he knew before. This is purchasing too dearly a species of information which can be easily gained conjointly with higher departments of composition. For those who make reading the basis of study, and follow our suggestions, correct spelling is as necessary a consequence as is pronunciation in the acquisition of the mother-tongue. By dictation, the professor teaches nothing to his pupils that they could not learn by themselves. It is so universally adopted, only because it is easily available, demanding, on the part of the teacher, little trouble, capacity, or information.

Premature exercises of pronunciation, forced in by the priority given to the art of speaking, have a still more pernicious effect than those which relate to orthography. They are primarily addressed to the *eye*, as they proceed from the letters to the sounds; whereas, on the contrary, a knowledge of the pronunciation should first be gained, in order to ascertain the value of the alphabetical characters which represent them. It is the inversion of the order in which the different branches of a language should be learned that has given rise to the practice of reading aloud, and to all those dissertations on the letters of the alphabet which serve as an introduction to nearly all grammars.

As an early initiation in oral reading, books have been contrived, in which the pronunciation of the foreign language is assimilated with that of the native, by alphabetical combinations in the latter. The attempt to spell words in one language as they are pronounced in another, must, in most cases, prove unsuccessful; for the pen can neither represent new sounds to the eye, nor mark the imperceptible shades of colloquial intonation. Every language has vowel sounds, articulations, and an accentuation peculiar to itself. Of the French vocal elements, for example, seven sounds and one articulation, are not in the English pronunciation, and cannot, therefore, be represented by English letters.* Such contrivances only familiarize the eye with a defective spelling of the foreign words.

There is nothing more common than to make beginners read aloud each phrase of the text before translating it. In Latin, which is pronounced by modern nations nearly the same as

* The French sounds represented by *ê*, *u*, *eû*, *an*, *in*, *on*, *un*, and the articulation of which *ill* is the sign, do not exist in the English pronunciation.

their own language, the previous reading has no inconvenience; it is even necessary, in order to unravel the inverted arrangement of its words, and to construe these conformably to the genius of the language into which the translation is to be made. The case is different as regards the modern languages of Europe, in which the words often assume the same order, but differ widely in their pronunciation. Without in any way helping to understand the text, this mode of proceeding inevitably leads to a defective pronunciation.

Alternately pronouncing and translating each sentence, constantly disjoins the subject, and thereby not only lessens the interest that the narrative might create, but also throws an obstacle in the way of making out the sense from the context. Besides, a beginner cannot attend at the same time to the pronunciation and the construction, both being new to him; he necessarily neglects the one while attending to the other. Finally, this practice forms habits contrary to the object most desirable in translating, the power of doing so at sight and without preparation.

In a class, reading aloud engages only one

person at a time, and leaves all the others for a great part of the time in a state of lamentable listlessness, or, which is still worse, if they listen, accustoms them to the more or less defective pronunciation of those who read. Reciting and correcting exercises in class are liable to a similar objection: they require the exclusive attention of the master for each pupil separately.

When reading aloud is practised at the commencement of the study, in the presence of an instructor, careful to correct every error of pronunciation, these recur so frequently that very little time remains for translation, which, at the outset, ought to be the only object of consideration. These difficulties would be only partially obviated if the professor himself, as is sometimes done, should pronounce every word or phrase before the pupil; for the ear cannot, on a first hearing, notice at once all the shades of difference which mark the vocal elements in a strange language, and especially the accent and quantity; these are so delicate that, to be perceived, they demand extreme sensibility of the organ, cultivated by long and patient practice in hearing.

With regard to the art of reading as an accomplishment, its acquisition is utterly impossible in a foreign language, so long as a person has not become so habituated to its pronunciation, as to have his mind completely free to give his attention exclusively to the author's thought. It is, moreover, of little service; for a person has rarely occasion to read in a foreign language to his own countrymen, and still less to foreigners. But, in one's own language, no pains should be spared in acquiring this accomplishment, which, though most useful and agreeable, is seldom possessed.

The adoption of these different processes is injurious to the teaching of languages, especially because it favors the ignorance and incapacity of those who resort to teaching, after having failed in other occupations. The exercises of memory, in which the master acts a merely passive part, are equally objectionable. Teachers are apt to resort exclusively to this faculty for various branches of instruction, although there is no need of any special exercise to call it into activity; for its action, like that of attention, is comprised in that of the other faculties. It is by no means unusual to see unfortunate children poring over vocabularies or other compilations, forced to learn by heart lists of words, conjugations, dialogues, passages of books, which they never turn to account for the expression of their thoughts.

The study of words as an introduction to a language, is a violation of the laws of nature, and leads to no useful result. One could read two or three volumes with interest, by means of interpretations in juxtaposition, in less time than would be consumed in painfully learning five or six hundred words as a preparation for reading. But this point has already been alluded to; we will now advert to dialogues and extracts as mnemonic lessons. In these the attention is directed solely to the words which are associated in the mind by their contiguity. By dint of repetition they are necessarily recalled in their order of succession, each word suggesting that which follows. The more frequently the lesson is repeated in the act of learning it, the easier is the recitation, the more also does the text escape analysis and the control of the will. Recitation is an exercise in oratorical delivery, not in the expression of one's own ideas.

The habit produced by the repetition of a text is diametrically opposed to the mental operation required for the expression of thought: speaking is an act of the judgment, reciting an act of the memory. The first consists in associating words with the ideas as these arise in the mind; the second in merely associating words with each other on the principle of contiguity. Incessant change of words and phraseology characterizes the one; immutability of form and order is the essence of the other. We command the former, we are slaves to the latter. In speaking, the attention is intent on ideas; in reciting, it is intent on words; in the former the words are subordinate to the ideas, in the latter the ideas are subordinate to the words, very often they are not taken into consideration at all; there is nothing so common with children as to repeat what they do not in the least understand. "To know by heart is not knowing," said Montaigne.

Dialogues, like extracts learned by rote, teach to recite, not to converse. Whatever be the number with which a learner has loaded his memory, he is only the tame repeater of another man's ideas; he is never called upon to express his own, and his power of conversing is regulated by the whim and peculiar notions of the compiler.

It is obvious that the art of speaking depends not so much on the recollection of a large number of dialogues as on the power of spontaneously constructing sentences suited to the ever-changing circumstances of social intercourse. Analogy, the power through the instrumentality of which command of expression is acquired, is therefore more effective than mere recollection of phraseology.

How can it be supposed that a dialogue, for example, between a lady and her dress-maker, written most likely by a man little conversant with the caprices of fashion, or with female attire, could serve as a type for all conversations between ladies and their dress-makers, despite the changes of fashion and whatever be the season of the year, the dispositions, ages, wants, taste, wealth of the parties, and innumerable other circumstances. The victims of this system, however, are generally spared the trouble of testing the usefulness of these dialogues; they generally forget them long before they have an opportunity to turn them to account.

Not only are these lessons of very little service, but, as they demand much time, and are very irksome, they can hardly fail to inspire aversion for study. They do not even cultivate the memory in any useful way, for the faculty of remembering words in a given order, serves no practical purpose, unless to actors in learning their parts.

No faculty can be exercised and improved generally by any particular process; its cultivation in one direction does not extend its power in another; thus persons, practised in musical modulations, have no superiority over others in catching the pronunciation and accent of foreign languages. If the sight be exercised on colors, it will not better appreciate forms or distances, and if exercised on either forms or distances, only a similar partial improvement will be produced. It is the same with the intellectual faculties. Their development is always in accordance with the means by which it is attained. The person who has been much engaged in learning mere words or passages of books will not, from that special exercise, possess greater power in recollecting facts, localities, dates, the subject-matter of a book or of a speech. In short, the practice of committing to memory words and phrases, gives to this faculty nothing more than an aptitude for parroting another man's words and phrases, and such an aptitude will never raise its possessor in the scale of intellect, or enable him to carry on more successfully the affairs of life. The mechanical memory of words should not be made a substitute for the intellectual memory of things.

All the time which a boy spends in learning by heart and reciting lessons is lost for the exercise of his judgment and for the practice of the language. In classes the great majority of its members remain unoccupied, awaiting their turn to be heard. As for the professor, what does he do? He listens, he does not teach. However extensive his knowledge may be, it is a dead letter to his pupils. He who, in his teaching, does not go beyond the books, is no professor.

The numerous tasks which, in the prevailing systems of instruction, young people often have to prepare for their instructor, allow them no time to practise reading in his absence, or the spoken language in his presence. They leave school, for the most part, without having entered upon any essential department of the study. They are given to understand that their labor is over when they begin to read aloud, and translate or parse the foreign language with fluency, when they have conjugated all the verbs, and repeated a volume of dialogues, when they have learned all the rules, and written all the exercises of their grammar; and yet nothing of all this is the language, the practical language.

These sad results are the more remarkable as we every day see young children acquire a second language abroad with a facility which would put to shame an adult who was learning the same language in the plenitude of his reason, who, having only to collect signs to be attached to the ideas he possesses, spends considerably more time in learning them than do these children in learning to speak the language, although the latter have to acquire every thing—the ideas as well as their signs. Nothing shows more obviously the fallacy of the methods pursued.

The easiest and most useful branch, the art of reading, they seldom acquire so as to turn it to advantage in after-life. Their study of it does not extend beyond the translation of a few volumes or fragments of volumes; and, consequently, there are very few who, after leaving school, ever open a book in a living language, unable as they are to read that language with ease or pleasure.

These are the sad fruits of a routine which, by confining learners exclusively to translation, incapacitates them from entering into the spirit of authors, or to appreciate their merit, and which, by frequently enforcing on them the practice of scrap-reading, leaves them lamentably ignorant of the foreign literature.

The routine of classical studies especially is deplorable in its consequences; it does not conform either to the laws of Nature or to the requirements of society, sets at naught spontaneity, curiosity, imitation, and analogy; overloads memory to the prejudice of judgment, reverses the order prescribed by reason, in passing from the signs to the things signified, from the rules of grammar to the facts of language, from the art of writing to the art of reading; nor does it fully secure the intellectual development aimed at by these studies, and keeps young people too long engaged on things of the past, to the exclusion of the knowledge which the progress of civilization has rendered indispensable.

We do not mean by these remarks to cast censure on the profession of teacher. The most enlightened among its members lament the present state of things as much as we do, but are unable to offer a remedy. So strong is the prejudice in favor of the course sanctioned by time and school-routine, that the head of a private school, or the professor who should wish to introduce a reform in this respect, would probably be exposed to great personal prejudice.

"Custom," says Rollin, "often exercises over minds a sort of tyranny which keeps them in bondage and hinders the use of reason, which, in these matters, is a surer guide than example, however authorized by time."

Of all the known methods there is not one in strict conformity with the process of nature or which furnishes the means of thoroughly acquiring a foreign language, in its fourfold application.

Dumarsais, Rollin, Pluche, Radonvilliers, and Lemare, authors of special treatises on the art of teaching languages, have presented very judicious suggestions on the matter; but, as they had exclusively in view the study of the dead languages, they suggested no means of effecting the oral exchange of ideas. The method of interlinear translations, advocated by some of them, as well as by Locke, however excellent and practical, can lead only to the understanding of the written language.

The imitation of a model-book, as recommended by Jacotot, certainly places the student in the right track; but it is a perversion of his principle, "All is in all," to limit, as he does, the knowledge of a language to the study of a single volume, and to force on his pupils a defective pronunciation, by insisting, as he does, on their committing this volume to memory at the very outset, when they are utterly ignorant of the pronunciation of the foreign tongue. This is not surely the way in which Nature proceeds. He initiates his pupils in the art of speaking by asking them questions on the text of this volume, which they are to answer by repeating the very words of the author. This repetition of words and phrases, drawn exclusively from one text, is assuredly insufficient. The subject-matter and the phraseology of his model-book, Telemachus, are also ill adapted for the purposes of ordinary conversation.

In the Ollendorff system, practice justly comes before theory; but the trivial phraseology of which its lessons are made up, and their recitation, afford no aid toward extempore speaking or the formation of a good style, despite the pretentious title of his book: "Method of learning to speak, read, and write German in six months." This title alone proves that Ollendorff did not even suspect that the art of understanding the spoken language could be taught.

Robertson's method, partly copied from Jacotot's, is not less barren in results. Rejecting the progressive order prescribed by Nature, it aims, from the outset, at the four arts simultaneously; hence his premature lessons of pronunciation, grammar, etymology, parsing, analytical and philological disquisitions, which constantly take the attention away from what is practically useful. The pupils have no other subject of study, in the whole course of this method, but a text still more restricted than that of Jacotot; and, far from recommending the reading of good authors, Mr. Robertson pretends, contrary to common sense, that the short Persian tale of three or four pages, on which his lessons turn, suffices for all the acquirements of the foreign language.

In short, neither these methods, nor any other that has come to our knowledge, secure the means of understanding foreigners when speaking their own language, and still less that of acquiring the power of thinking in that idiom, a power essential to its thorough mastery.

The diversity of lights in which linguistic instruction is viewed, owing to the absence of a rational classification, has naturally produced a corresponding diversity in the mode of effecting it. Every teacher, in entering on his profession, bewildered by all these processes, many of which are in direct opposition to one another, has to contrive a method for himself, or he must blindly follow the routine which often has no other recommendation than its antiquity.

This appeal to our fathers in what regards education keeps the mind in bondage, and is an obstacle to progress: they are our juniors in the world. We have our own experience in addition to theirs, and start in life with greater advantages; we consequently ought to know more, and cannot make their notions or opinions the standard of our conduct. It is time to reject the worn-out machinery of our forefathers. Let us apply to mind, as we have done to matter, new powers and new processes. Let a rational system of learning languages bring men of all nations into communion, as steam has brought them into contact.*

* We refer the reader to the work mentioned in the preface for more ample information on the system here briefly sketched, and on the processes which constitute its practical application.

THE END.

# LIST OF WORKS

# PUBLISHED BY D. APPLETON & CO.,

## 90, 92 & 94 GRAND ST., NEW YORK.

*A Descriptive Catalogue, with full titles and prices, may be had gratuitously on application.*

About's Roman Question.
Adams' Boys at Home.
—— Edgar Clifton.
Addison's Spectator. 6 vols.
Adler's German and English Dictionary.
—— Abridged do. do. do.
—— German Reader.
—— " Literature.
—— Ollendorff for Learning German.
—— Key to the Exercises.
—— Iphigenia in Tauris.
After Icebergs with a Painter.
Agnel's Book of Chess.
Aguilar's Home Influence.
—— Mother's Recompense.
—— Days of Bruce. 2 vols.
—— Home Scenes.
—— Woman's Friendship.
—— Women of Israel. 2 vols.
—— Vale of Cedars.
Ahn's French Method.
—— Spanish Grammar.
—— A Key to same.
—— German Method. 1 vol.
Or, separately—First Course. 1 vol.
Second " 1 vol.
Aids to Faith. A series of Essays, by Various Writers.
Aikin's British Poets. From Chaucer to the Present Time. 3 vols.
Album for Postage Stamps.
Albums of Foreign Galleries; in 7 folios.
Alden's Elements of Intellectual Philosophy.
Alison's Miscellaneous Essays.
Allen's Mechanics of Nature.
Alsop's Charms of Fancy.
Amelia's Poems.
American Poets (Gems from the).
American Eloquence. A Collection of Speeches and Addresses. 2 vols.
American System of Education:
1. Hand-Book of Anglo-Saxon Root-Words.
2. Hand-Book of Anglo-Saxon Derivatives.
American System of Education:
3. Hand-Book of Engrafted Words.
Anderson's Mercantile Correspondence.
Andrews' New French Instructor.
—— A Key to the above.
Annals of San Francisco.
Antisell on Coal Oils.
Anthon's Law Student.
Appletons' New American Cyclopædia of Useful Knowledge. 16 vols.
—— Annual Cyclopædia, and Register of Important Events for 1861, '62, '63, '64, '65.
—— Cyclopædia of Biography, Foreign and American.
—— Cyclopædia of Drawing.
The same in parts:
Topographical Drawing.
Perspective and Geometrical Drawing.
Shading and Shadows.
Drawing Instruments and their Uses.
Architectural Drawing and Design.
Mechanical Drawing and Design.
—— Dictionary of Mechanics and Engineering. 2 large vols.
—— Railway Guide.
—— American Illustrated Guide Book. 1 vol.
Do. do., separately:
1. Eastern and Middle States, and British Provinces. 1 vol.
2. Southern and Western States, and the Territories. 1 vol.
—— Companion Hand-Book of Travel.
Arabian Nights' Entertainments.
Arnold's (S. G.) History of the State of Rhode Island. 2 vols.
Arnold's (Dr.) History of Rome.
—— Modern History.
Arnold's Classical Series:
—— First Latin Book.
—— First and Second Latin Book and Grammar.
—— Latin Prose Composition.
—— Cornelius Nepos.
—— First Greek Book.
—— Greek Prose Composition Book, 1.

Arnold's Greek Prose Composition Book, 2.
—— Greek Reading Book.
Arthur's (T. S.) Tired of Housekeeping.
Arthur's (W.) Successful Merchant.
At Anchor; or, A Story of our Civil War.
Atlantic Library. 7 vols. in case.
Attaché in Madrid.
Aunt Fanny's Story Book.
—— Mitten Series. 6 vols. in case.
—— Night Cap Series. 6 vols. in case.

Badois' English Grammar for Frenchmen.
—— A Key to the above.
Baine's Manual of Composition and Rhetoric.
Bakewell's Great Facts
Baldwin's Flush Times.
—— Party Leaders.
Balmanno's Pen and Pencil.
Bank Law of the United States.
Barrett's Beauty for Ashes.
Bartlett's U. S. Explorations. 2 vols.
——— Cheap edition. 2 vols. in 1.
Barwell's Good in Every Thing.
Bassnett's Theory of Storms.
Baxley's West Coast of America and Hawaiian Islands.
Beach's Pelayo. An Epic.
Beall (John Y.), Trial of.
Beauties of Sacred Literature.
Beauties of Sacred Poetry.
Beaumont and Fletcher's Works. 2 vols.
Belem's Spanish Phrase Book.
Bello's Spanish Grammar (in Spanish).
Benedict's Run Through Europe.
Benton on the Dred Scott Case.
—— Thirty Years' View. 2 vols.
—— Debates of Congress. 16 vols.
Bertha Percy. By Margaret Field. 12mo.
Bertram's Harvest of the Sea. Economic and Natural History of Fishes.
Bessie and Jessie's Second Book.
Beza's Novum Testamentum.
Bibles in all styles of bindings and various prices.
Bible Stories, in Bible Language.
Black's General Atlas of the World.
Bloomfield's Farmer's Boy.
Blot's What to Eat, and How to Cook it.
Blue and Gold Poets. 6 vols. in case.
Boise's Greek Exercises.
—— First Three Books of Xenophon's Anabasis.
Bojesen's Greek and Roman Antiquities.
Book of Common Prayer. Various prices.
Boone's Life and Adventures.
Bourne's Catechism of the Steam Engine.
—— Hand-Book of the Steam Engine.
—— Treatise on the Steam Engine.
Boy's Book of Modern Travel.
—— Own Toy Maker.
Bradford's Peter the Great.
Bradley's (Mary E.) Douglass Farm.
Bradley's (Chas.) Sermons.
Brady's Christmas Dream.
Breakfast, Dinner, and Tea.
British Poets. From Chaucer to the Present Time. 8 large vols.
British Poets. Cabinet Edition. 15 vols.
Brooks' Ballads and Translations.
Brown, Jones, and Robinson's Tour.
Bryan's English Grammar for Germans.
Bryant & Stratton's Commercial Law.
Bryant's Poems, Illustrated.
—— Poems. 2 vols.
—— Thirty Poems.
—— Poems. Blue and Gold.
—— Letters from Spain.
Buchanan's Administration.
Buckle's Civilization in England. 2 vols.
—— Essays.
Bunyan's Divine Emblems.
Burdett's Chances and Changes.
—— Never Too Late.
Burgess' Photograph Manual. 12mo.
Burnett (James R.) on the Thirty-nine Articles.
Burnett (Peter H.), The Path which led a Protestant Lawyer to the Catholic Church.
Burnouf's Gramatica Latina.
Burns' (Jabez) Cyclopædia of Sermons.
Burns' (Robert) Poems.
Burton's Cyclopædia of Wit and Humor. 2 vols.
Butler's Martin Van Buren.
Butler's (F.) Spanish Teacher.
Butler's (S.) Hudibras.
Butler's (T. B.) Guide to the Weather.
Butler's (Wm. Allen) Two Millions.
Byron Gallery. The Gallery of Byron Beauties.
—— Poetical Works.
—— Life and Letters.
—— Works. Illustrated.

Cœleb's Laws and Practice of Whist.
Cæsar's Commentaries.
Caird's Prairie Farming.
Calhoun's Works and Speeches. 6 vols.
Campbell's (Thos.) Gertrude of Wyoming.
—— Poems.
Campbell (Judge) on Shakespeare.
Canot, Life of Captain.
Carlyle's (Thomas) Essays.
Carreno's Manual of Politeness.

Carreno's Compendio del Manual de Urbanidad.
Casseday's Poetic Lacon.
Cavendish's Laws of Whist.
Cervantes' Don Quixote, in Spanish.
—— Don Quixote, in English.
César L'Histoire de Jules, par S. M. I. Napoleon III. Vol. I., with Maps and Portrait. (French.)
Cheap Edition, without Maps and Portrait.
Maps and Portrait, for cheap edition, in envelopes.
Champlin's English Grammar.
—— Greek Grammar.
Chase on the Constitution and Canons.
Chaucer's Poems.
Chevalier on Gold.
Children's Holidays.
Child's First History.
Choquet's French Composition.
—— French Conversation.
Cicero de Officiis.
Chittenden's Report of the Peace Convention.
—— Select Orations.
Clarke's (D. S.) Scripture Promises.
Clarke's (Mrs. Cowden) Iron Cousin.
Clark's (H. J.) Mind in Nature.
Cleaveland and Backus' Villas and Cottages.
Cleveland's (H. W. S.) Hints to Riflemen.
Cloud Crystals. A Snow Flake Album.
Cobb's (J. B.) Miscellanies.
Coe's Spanish Drawing Cards. 10 parts.
Coe's Drawing Cards. 10 parts.
Colenso on the Pentateuch. 2 vols.
—— On the Romans.
Coleridge's Poems.
Collins' Amoor.
Collins' (T. W.) Humanics.
Collet's Dramatic French Reader.
Comings' Physiology.
—— Companion to Physiology.
Comment on Parle a Paris.
Congreve's Comedy.
Continental Library. 6 vols. in case.
Cooke's Life of Stonewall Jackson.
Cookery, by an American Lady.
Cooley's Cyclopædia of Receipts.
Cooper's Mount Vernon.
Copley's Early Friendship.
—— Poplar Grove.
Cornell's First Steps in Geography.
—— Primary Geography.
—— Intermediate Geography.
—— Grammar School Geography.
—— High School Geography and Atlas.
—— High School Geography.
—— " " Atlas.
—— Map Drawing. 12 maps in case.
—— Outline Maps, with Key. 13 maps in portfolio.
—— Or, the Key, separately.

Cornwall on Music.
Correlation and Conservation of Forces.
Cortez' Life and Adventures.
Cotter on the Mass and Rubrics.
Cottin's Elizabeth; or, the Exiles of Siberia.
Cousin Alice's Juveniles.
Cousin Carrie's Sun Rays.
—— Keep a Good Heart.
Cousin's Modern Philosophy. 2 vols.
—— On the True and Beautiful.
—— Only Romance.
Coutan's French Poetry.
Covell's English Grammar.
Cowles' Exchange Tables.
Cowper's Homer's Iliad.
—— Poems.
Cox's Eight Years in Congress, from 1857 to 1865.
Coxe's Christian Ballads.
Creasy on the English Constitution.
Crisis (The).
Crosby's (A.) Geometry.
Crosby's (H.) Œdipus Tyrannus.
Crosby's (W. H.) Quintus Curtius Rufus.
Crowe's Linny Lockwood.
Curry's Volunteer Book.
Cust's Invalid's Book.
Cyclopædia of Commercial and Business Anecdotes. 2 vols.

D'Abrantes' Memoires of Napoleon. 2 vols.
Dairyman's (The) Daughter.
Dana's Household Poetry.
Darwin's Origin of Species.
Dante's Poems.
Dasent's Popular Tales from the Norse.
Davenport's Christian Unity and its Recovery.
Dawson's Archaia.
De Belem's Spanish Phrase-Book.
De Fivas' Elementary French Reader.
—— Classic French Reader.
De Foe's Robinson Crusoe.
De Girardin's Marguerite.
—— Stories of an Old Maid.
De Hart on Courts Martial.
De L'Ardeche's History of Napoleon.
De Peyrac's Comment on Parle.
De Staël's Corinne, ou L'Italie.
De Veitelle's Mercantile Dictionary.
De Vere's Spanish Grammar.
Dew's Historical Digest.
Dickens's (Charles) Works. Original Illustrations. 24 vols.
Dies Irae and Stabat Mater, bound together.
Dies Irae, alone, and Stabat Mater, alone.
Dix's (John A.) Winter in Madeira.
—— Speeches and Addresses. 2 vols.

Dix's (Rev. M.) Lost Unity of the Christian World.
Dr. Oldham at Greystones, and his Talk there.
Doane's Works. 4 vols.
Downing's Rural Architecture.
Dryden's Poems.
Dunlap's Spirit History of Man.
Dusseldorf Gallery, Gems from the.
Dwight on the Study of Art.
Ebony Idol (The).
Ede's Management of Steel.
Edith Vaughan's Victory.
Egloffstein's Geology and Physical Geography of Mexico.
Eichhorn's German Grammar.
Elliot's Fine Work on Birds. 7 parts, or in 1 vol.
Ellsworth's Text-Book of Penmanship.
Ely's Journal.
Enfield's Indian Corn; its Value, Culture, and Uses.
Estvan's War Pictures.
Evans' History of the Shakers.
Evelyn's Life of Mrs. Godolphin.
Everett's Mount Vernon Papers.

Fables, Original and Selected.
Farrar's History of Free Thought.
Faustus.
Fay's Poems.
Fénélon's Telemaque.
——— The same, in 2 vols.
——— Telemachus.
Field's Bertha Percy.
Field's (M.) City Architecture.
Figuier's World before the Deluge.
Fireside Library. 8 vols. in case.
First Thoughts.
Fiji and the Fijians.
Flint's Physiology of Man.
Florian's William Tell.
Flower Pictures.
Fontana's Italian Grammar.
Foote's Africa and the American Flag.
Foresti's Italian Extracts.
Four Gospels (The).
Franklin's Man's Cry and God's Gracious Answer.
Frieze's Tenth and Twelfth Books of Quintilian.
Fullerton's (Lady G.) Too Strange Not to be True.
Funny Story Book.

Garland's Life of Randolph.
Gaskell's Life of Brontë. 2 vols.
The same, cheaper edition, in 1 vol.
George Ready.
Gerard's French Readings.
Gertrude's Philip Randolph.
Gesenius' Hebrew Grammar.
Ghostly Colloquies.
Gibbes' Documentary History. 3 vols.
Gibbons' Banks of New York.
Gilfillan's Literary Portraits.
Gillespie on Land Surveying.
Girardin on Dramatic Literature.
Goadby's Text-Book of Physiology.
Goethe's Iphigenia in Tauris.
Goldsmith's Essays.
——— Vicar of Wakefield.
Gosse's Evenings with the Microscope.
Goulburn's Office of the Holy Communion.
——— Idle Word.
——— Manual of Confirmation.
——— Sermons.
——— Study of the Holy Scriptures.
——— Thoughts on Personal Religion.
Gould's (E. S.) Comedy.
Gould's (W. M.) Zephyrs.
Graham's English Synonymes.
Grandmamma Easy's Toy Books.
Grandmother's Library. 6 vols. in case.
Grand's Spanish Arithmetic.
Grant's Report on the Armies of the United States 1864-'65.
Grauet's Portuguese Grammar.
Grayson's Theory of Christianity.
Greek Testament.
Greene's (F. H.) Primary Botany.
—— Class-Book of Botany.
Greene's (G. W.) Companion to Ollendorff.
—— First Lessons in French.
—— First Lessons in Italian.
—— Middle Ages.
Gregory's Mathematics.
Griffin on the Gospel.
Griffith's Poems.
Griswold's Republican Court.
——— Sacred Poets.
Guizot's (Madame) Tales.
Guizot's (M.) Civilization in Europe. 4 vols.
—— School edition. 1 vol.
—— New Edition, on tinted paper. 4 vols.
Gurowski's America and Europe.
——— Russia as it is.

Hadley's Greek Grammar.
Hahn's Greek Testament.
Hall's (B. H.) Eastern Vermont.
Hall's (C. H.) Notes on the Gospels. 2 vols.
Hall's (E. H.) Guide to the Great West.
Halleck's Poems.
—— Poems. Pocket size, blue and gold.
—— Young America.
Halleck's (H. W.) Military Science.
Hamilton's (Sir Wm.) Philosophy.
Hamilton's (A.) Writings. 6 vols.

Hand-Books on Education.
Hand-Book of Anglo-Saxon Root-Words.
Hand-Book of Anglo-Saxon Derivatives.
Hand-Book of the Engrafted Words.
Handy-Book of Property Law.
Happy Child's Library. 18 vols. in case.
Harkness' First Greek Book.
—— Latin Grammar.
—— First Latin Book.
—— Second "
—— Latin Reader.
Hase's History of the Church.
Haskell's Housekeeper's Encyclopædia.
Hassard's Life of Archbishop Hughes.
—— Wreath of Beauty.
Haupt on Bridge Construction.
Haven's Where There's a Will There's a Way.
—— Patient Waiting no Loss.
—— Nothing Venture Nothing Have.
—— Out of Debt Out of Danger.
—— Contentment Better than Wealth.
—— No Such Word as Fail.
—— All's Not Gold that Glitters.
—— A Place for Everything, and Everything in its Place.
—— Loss and Gain.
—— Pet Bird.
—— Home Series of Juvenile Books. 8 vols. in case.
Haven (Memoir of Alice B.).
Hazard on the Will.
Hecker's Questions of the Soul.
Hemans' Poems. 2 vols.
—— Songs of the Affections.
Henck's Field-Book for Engineers.
Henry on Human Progress.
Herbert's Poems.
Here and There.
Herodotus, by Johnson (in Greek).
Herodotus, by Rawlinson (in English). 4 vols.
Heydenreich's German Reader.
Hickok's Rational Cosmology.
—— Rational Psychology.
History of the Rebellion, Military and Naval. Illustrated.
Hoffman's Poems.
Holcombe's Leading Cases.
—— Law of Dr. and Cr.
—— Letters in Literature.
Holly's Country Seats.
Holmes' (M. A.) Tempest and Sunshine.
—— English Orphans.
Holmes' (A.) Parties and Principles.
Homes of American Authors.
Homer's Iliad.
Hooker's Complete Works. 2 vols.
Hoppin's Notes.
Horace, edited by Lincoln.
Howitt's Child's Verse-Book.
—— Juvenile Tales. 14 vols. in case.
How's Historical Shakspearian Reader.
—— Shakspearian Reader.
Huc's Tartary and China.
Hudson's Life and Adventures.
Humboldt's Letters.
Hunt's (C. H.) Life of Livingston.
Hunt's (F. W.) Historical Atlas.
Huntington's Lady Alice.
Hutton's Mathematics.
Huxley's Man's Place in Nature.
—— Origin of Species.

Iconographic Encyclopædia. 6 vols.—4 Text and 2 Plates.
Or, separately:
The Countries and Cities of the World. 2 vols.
The Navigation of all Ages. 2 vols.
The Art of Building in Ancient and Modern Times. 2 vols.
The Religions of Ancient and Modern Times. 2 vols.
The Fine Arts Illustrated. 2 vols.
Technology Illustrated. 2 vols.
Internal Revenue Law.
Iredell's Life. 2 vols.
Italian Comedies.

Jacobs' Learning to Spell.
—— The same, in two parts.
Jaeger's Class-Book of Zoology.
James' (J. A.) Young Man.
James' (H.) Logic of Creation.
James' (G. P. R.) Adrien.
Jameson's (Mrs.) Art Works.
—— Legends of Saints and Martyrs. 2 vols.
—— Legends of the Monastic Orders.
—— Legends of the Madonna.
—— History of Our Lord. 2 vols.
Jarvis' Reply to Milner.
Jay on American Agriculture.
Jeffers on Gunnery.
Jeffrey's (F.) Essays.
Johnson's Meaning of Words.
Johnson's (Samuel) Rasselas.
Johnston's Chemistry of Common Life. 2 vols.

Kavanagh's Adele.
—— Beatrice.
—— Daisy Burns.
—— Grace Lee.
—— Madeleine.
—— Nathalie.
—— Rachel Gray.
—— Seven Years.
—— Queen Mab.
—— Women of Christianity.
Keats' Poems.

Keep a Good Heart.
Keightley's Mythology.
Keil's Fairy Stories.
Keith (Memoir of Caroline P.)
Kendrick's Greek Ollendorff.
Kenny's Manual of Chess.
Kinglake's Crimean War. Vols. 1 and 2.
Kirke White's Poems.
Kirkland's Life of Washington.
A Cheaper Edition, for Schools.
Knowles' Orlean Lamar.
Kœppen's Middle Ages.
—— Separately—Middle Ages, 2 vols.
—— Atlas.
Kohlrausch's History of Germany.
Kuhner's Greek Grammar.

Lafever's Beauties of Architecture.
Lady Alice.
Lamartine's Confidential Disclosures.
—— History of Turkey. 3 vols.
Lancelott's Queens of England, and their Times. 2 vols.
Landon's (L. E.) Complete Works.
Latham's English Language.
Layard's Nineveh. Illustrated.
—— Cheap edition. Without Illustrations.
Learning to Spell.
Le Brun's Telemaque.
Lecky's Rise and Influence of Rationalism. 2 vols.
Le Sage's Adventures of Gil Blas. 1 vol.
—— Gil Blas, in Spanish.
Letter Writer.
Letters from Rome.
Lewes' (G. H.) History of Philosophy. 2 vols.
—— In 1 vol.
—— Physiology of Common Life.
Library of Travel and Adventure. 3 vols. in case.
Library for my Young Countrymen. 9 vols. in case.
Libro Primario de Ortografia.
Liebig's Laws of Husbandry.
Life of Man Symbolized by the Months of the Year.
Light and Darkness
Lights and Shadows of New York Picture Galleries.
Lindsay's Poems.
Linn's Life and Services.
Little Builder.
Little Engineer.
Livy, with English Notes.
Logan's Château Frissac.
Looking Glass for the Mind.
Lord's Poems.
—— Christ in Hades: a Poem.
Louise.
Lunt's Origin of the Late War.
Lyell's Elements of Geology.
Lyell's Principles of Geology.
Lyra Americana.
Lyra Anglicana.

Macaulay's Essays. 1 vol.
—— Essays. 7 vols.
—— Essays. A New and Revised Edition, on tinted paper. 6 vols.
Mackintosh's (Sir James) Essays.
Madge.
Mahan's Answer to Colenso.
—— Numerals of Scripture.
Mahon's England. 2 vols.
Maiu's Novum Testamentum Græce.
Mandeville's New Series of Readers.
1. Primary Reader.
2. Second Reader.
3. Third Reader.
4. Fourth Reader.
5. Fifth Reader.
Mandeville's Course of Reading.
—— Reading and Oratory.
—— First Spanish Reader.
—— Second Spanish Reader.
—— Third Spanish Reader.
Magnall's Historical Questions.
Man's Cry and God's Gracious Answer.
Manners' At Home and Abroad.
—— Sedgemoor.
Manning's Temporal Mission of the Holy Ghost.
—— The Reunion of Christendom.
Manual of Matrimony.
Markham's History of England.
Marrayat's Africa.
—— Masterman Ready.
—— Popular Novels. 12 vols.
—— A New and Revised Edition, printed on tinted paper 12 vols.
Marryat's Settlers in Canada.
Marshall's (E. C.) Book of Oratory.
—— First Book of Oratory.
Marshall's (T. W.) Notes on Episcopacy.
Marsh's Double Entry Book-keeping.
—— Single Entry Book-keeping.
—— Bank Book-keeping.
—— Book-keeping (in Spanish).
—— Blank Books for Double Entry. 6 books in set.
—— Do. for Single Entry. 6 books in set.
Martha's Hooks and Eyes.
Martineau's Crofton Boys.
—— Peasant and Prince.
Mary Lee.
Mary Staunton.
Mathews on Whist.
Mayhew's Illustrated Horse Docto
May's Bertram Noel.
—— Louis' School Days.
—— Mortimer's College Life.
—— Sunshine of Greystone.
McCormick's Visit to Sebastopol.

## MARCEL ON THE STUDY OF LANGUAGES.*

In most of the American colleges which include the modern languages as a part of their curriculum the mode of instruction in that department is the same as that which is applied to the study of the classics. The main object in both cases is not so much to give a practical mastery of the languages that are studied as to enable the student to appreciate and enjoy the productions of their literature, and to refer with ease to the authority of their writers in the various branches of learning. In consequence of this, few of our college students are able to speak and write the living languages of Europe with facility, or, in fact, to read the works that are written in them, without the more or less conscious intervention of their own language. They seldom attain the habit of directly connecting the words of a foreign tongue with the ideas which they represent; and, without the power of thinking in the language, are utterly at a loss to apply it for purposes of conversation. Doubtless it is a great advantage to understand a language sufficiently to read and translate the masterpieces of its literature. An acquaintance with the written language of Germany, especially, gives a key to profuse treasures of knowledge, which well repays the labor of years for its attainment, although for all the interests of social life it remains no less exclusively a dead language than Hebrew or Greek.

But with the progress of international intercourse a familiarity with foreign languages for purposes of business and conversation becomes a necessity. The number of American travelers in Europe is almost incredible; but without the ability to converse freely with the inhabitants a European tour loses a great part of its value and interest. The foreigner in a social circle of Europe who tries in vain to catch the import of the conversation finds himself in an awkward position; and, though perhaps able to instruct the natives in the literature of their mother-tongue, is more like a schoolboy than a traveler.

The author of this work, who is an ac- complished philologist of France and man of rare practical sense, as well as of admirable literary culture, has clearly perceived the chief difficulty of foreign travelers, and has developed a method of study which will give them the command of the spoken language with the same freedom and facility with which they are now able to enjoy the perusal of its literary works. After the pupil has made some progress in reading, for the acquisition of which M. Marcel presents several valuable directions, the attention is given to the cultivation of the ear, without forcing upon his unpracticed tongue the enunciation of sounds with whose significance he has not yet become familiar. A series of exercises intended to train the ear to the immediate comprehension of spoken words and phrases takes the place of premature attempts at pronunciation. By this simple process the pupil is initiated into the meaning of the vocal sounds which compose the spoken language, just as the infant learns the meaning of words in his native tongue from their constant repetition by father, mother, nurse, doting aunts, and admiring uncles, before the organs of speech are capable of distinct and connected articulation. But in the usual method of teaching adults the comprehension of the spoken language is not even regarded as a distinct art. There is not even a term by which to express it; and, in order to set forth the true principles of learning a language, the author has been obliged to attach a new signification to the words "hearing and audition." By the usual methods the pupil is left almost entirely without the power of understanding oral expression. The organ of hearing remains in complete inaction, or is only exercised on detached words and phrases. The ear untaught by the teacher's voice cannot, in the usual rapidity of speech, recognize the foreign words, however familiar they may be to the eye. This is the chief obstacle to conversation with those already familiar with the written language. But the same method by which the ear is formed to the articulate sounds of the mother tongue is applicable to their case. If followed with ordinary industry and intelligence, the pupil would be enabled to seize the meaning of the words and acquire the foreign pronunciation as easily as his own.

The difficulty of understanding a foreign language when spoken is often ascribed to the rapidity of pronunciation. Most persons, for instance, think that the French language is spoken faster than the English. But this is far from being the case. The English is spoken considerably quicker than the French; and this arises, as M. Marcel distinctly shows, from a difference of kind in the pronunciation of the languages. The elements of pronunciation are vocal sounds and articulations, which are represented in writing by vowels and consonants. The essence of vocal sounds is quantity, by which they admit of duration. Vocal articulation, on the other hand, with few exceptions, are instantaneous and cannot be prolonged. When a consonant is placed after a vowel it generally shortens it. Thus the long syllables *e, we, fi, no,* become short by adding consonants to them—*met, wet, fit, not.* Now in glish, consonants usually form the end syllables; and hence rapidity of utterce is the necessary consequence. In ench it is the other way. Consonants t but a secondary part, and are often ent. The spoken words end, in reality, th vowel sounds, although consonants minate their written representatives. e vowels which contribute so much to gthen the words are pronounced full, in ench, as if every syllable were accent-; and hence results a slow and steady onunciation.

We have pointed out but a single ture which shows the great practical lity of M. Marcel's method. But his views no less intelligent and suggestive in other branches of the study of langes. No one can peruse his work withreceiving fresh light on a most impor- department of education. But it is cipally for the throng of "fair women brave men" who frequent the capitals of Europe from this country that this little volume must prove a Godsend in opening the mouth of the dumb and unstopping the ears that are practically deaf. A forcible test of the excellence of M. Marcel's system is the perfect command which he has gained of the English language. The style of his book is not only singularly free from the traces of foreign idiom; but exhibits a facility, power, and nicety of expression which might well be envied by the most accomplished English writers.

www.ingramcontent.com/pod-product-compliance
Lightning Source LLC
LaVergne TN
LVHW050516100826
845148LV00002B/360

* 9 7 8 1 4 2 5 5 2 1 0 7 3 *